Routledge Revivals

The Real World of the Small Business Owner

Small businessmen and entrepreneurs came firmly back in fashion when this book was first published in 1980. As the Western economies moved into recession, many governments, particularly Mrs Thatcher's administration, looked to the entrepreneurial spirit of the small businessman to rejuvenate and revitalise Western society.

Stripping away the political rhetoric, this book provides a serious social portrait of the small businessman in the economy at the time in which this book was written. Based upon extensive original research, the detailed analyses focuses on the key issues in the small businessmen's life. At a time when there was much argument about the motivation and will to work for Western society, this study of the traditional custodians of capitalism is particularly relevant. Above all it shows how the historical values of the small businessman have survived in the changed circumstances of the advanced economies.

The Real World of the Small Business Owner

Richard Scase and Robert Goffee

Routledge
Taylor & Francis Group

First published in 1980
by Croom Helm

This edition first published in 2015 by Routledge
2 Park Square, Milton Park, Abingdon, Oxon, OX14 4RN
and by Routledge
711 Third Avenue, New York, NY 10017

Routledge is an imprint of the Taylor & Francis Group, an informa business

© 1980 Richard Scase and Robert Goffee

The rights of Richard Scase and Robert Goffee to be identified as authors of this work has been asserted by him in accordance with sections 77 and 78 of the Copyright, Designs and Patents Act 1988.

All rights reserved. No part of this book may be reprinted or reproduced or utilised in any form or by any electronic, mechanical, or other means, now known or hereafter invented, including photocopying and recording, or in any information storage or retrieval system, without permission in writing from the publishers.

Publisher's Note
The publisher has gone to great lengths to ensure the quality of this reprint but points out that some imperfections in the original copies may be apparent.

Disclaimer
The publisher has made every effort to trace copyright holders and welcomes correspondence from those they have been unable to contact.

A Library of Congress record exists under LC control number: 81100047

ISBN 13: 978-1-138-82943-5 (hbk)
ISBN 13: 978-1-315-73778-2 (ebk)
ISBN 13: 978-1-138-82944-2 (pbk)

The Real World of the Small Business Owner

RICHARD SCASE AND ROBERT GOFFEE

CROOM HELM LONDON

© 1980 Richard Scase and Robert Goffee
Croom Helm Ltd, 2-10 St John's Road, London SW11

British Library Cataloguing in Publication Data

Scase, Richard
   The real world of the small business owner.
   1. Small business – Great Britain
   2. Businessmen – Great Britain
   I. Goffee, Robert
   338.6'42'0941   HD2346.G7
   ISBN 0-7099-0452-5

Printed in Great Britain by
Biddles Ltd, Guildford, Surrey

CONTENTS

PREFACE

This book is written as a contribution to the popular debate about small business owners and the role of their enterprises within the modern economy. On the basis of a series of interviews, it explores the reasons why people start their own enterprises and the problems which they face as they expand. It discusses the managerial and organisational aspects of small businesses and the means whereby they cope with market circumstances. The role of taxation is considered in its effects on personal incentive and the growth of enterprises. Business owners' life-styles are described as well as their attitudes towards the state, the economy and trade unions. We have tried to present our argument and findings in a straightforward and uncomplicated manner — the book is not intended for the specialist in search of fundamental theory. A more theoretical discussion of our investigation will be published in *The Entrepreneurial Middle Class.*

The study was financed by the Social Science Research Council. The book itself has benefited considerably from the editorial skills and incisive observations of David Croom. In addition, we are grateful to Caryle Dean, Joan Hales, Sally Hewett and Avril Leech for their secretarial services. Finally, we owe special thanks to all those business owners who so openly described for us their personal experiences.

R.S. and R.G.

1 THE 'CRISIS' AND THE ROLE OF SMALL BUSINESSES

Business owners and entrepreneurs have again become popular figures after years of neglect. This is because they are seen to offer a solution to many of the problems confronting Western economies. According to several contemporary assumptions – many of which are highly questionable – we have become 'over-governed' by an increasingly powerful state bureaucracy so that social, personal and job security is now more important than the relentless pursuit of profit. Business proprietors, entrepreneurs and 'self-made' men, on the other hand, are regarded as people who are prepared to be self-reliant and to take the risks necessary for a dynamic economy. Indeed, so it is often argued, if only there was a greater spirit of entrepreneurship, more business enterprises would be created and, consequently, greater job opportunities and less unemployment. Furthermore, this same entrepreneurship would contribute to a culture emphasising self-reliance and personal responsibility such that governments could increasingly withdraw from economic management and the provision of a wide range of personal, social and welfare services. For many, then, the example set by entrepreneurs offers a solution to the institutional, attitudinal and cultural ills of present-day Western societies. Thus, it is necessary to return to the core values of Western capitalism, represented as they are by these people.

On the other hand, there are those who remain totally unconvinced by such arguments; indeed, such views are often regarded as downright reactionary. Yet these values have a much wider appeal than conventional liberal opinion would allow and not merely among core supporters of Margaret Thatcher or Ronald Reagan; in other words, rugged individualism continues to persist as a strong undercurrent throughout the whole of the Western world. It explains the widespread hostility towards government intervention, the welfare state and the collectivism of trade union movements and social democratic parties. Further, it accounts for much of the resentment directed towards the unemployed and to various low-income groups; individuals should be responsible for their own personal circumstances.

The popularity of these values is perhaps most evidently reflected in the economic and social polices of the British Conservative Govern-

ment elected in 1979, which explicitly regards them as a set of principles around which to rejuvenate the economy. The economic strategy of the Conservative Government is based upon certain assumptions
about personal incentive, human behaviour and economic motivation
that are steeped in notions of individualism and self-help. Sir Keith
Joseph, the Minister for Industry, for example, has argued that the
British economy will only be revived if entrepreneurship is more adequately rewarded. By this he means that an economic climate must be
created so that people will be prepared to take risks in order to create
and develop business enterprises. People must be left to stand on their
own two feet by severely restricting the protection and security offered
by the state. Further, they must be satisfactorily rewarded for the
economic risks they are prepared to take. This requires a reduction in
the level of direct taxation since, in addition to increasing the incentives for entrepreneurship, resources must be retained for the purposes
of further investment. Consequently, employment and economic
growth will be generated thereby resolving many of the nation's problems. Every attempt, then, must be made to re-emphasise the attractions of classical capitalism.

This whole approach is appropriately summed up in the Conservative Party pamphlet, *Small Business, Big Future*,

> It has rarely been as difficult to start or expand a business, or to
> hand it on to one's children as a going concern. For many, the
> pressure of bureaucracy and growth of controls have made their
> once-prized independence a burden too heavy to be worth carrying
> for much longer, while tax is destroying the incentive to bear it.
> Hope is being strangled and as a result those indispensable qualities
> of imagination, enterprise and drive are being stifled ... The aim
> must be to change the atmosphere and environment for the busi-
> ness community, to create anew conditions in which men and
> women of independent spirit will see it as worth their while to use
> their skill and enthusiasm to start or expand profitable enterprises.
> This must be the goal for all businesses of whatever size, and the
> whole of Conservative economic strategy should have that purpose
> ... More than one job in three outside the public sector is in small
> businesses. If they were encouraged to do so they could become the
> main source for new jobs.[1]

If nothing else, this is a new direction by comparison with the economic policies of successive governments during the post-war decades.

Over this period, the problems of the British economy have remained stubbornly the same – low economic growth, low investment, limited increases in productivity and outdated factories and machinery. But if the diagnoses of the 1950s and 1960s led to similar observations, the suggested remedies were very different to those of the 'new' economic strategy currently pursued by the Conservative Government.

In the 1960s, small businesses were generally regarded as a relic of the past. Economists and politicians were agreed that the development of modern complex technological processes required large-scale units of production if only because of the economies of scale. Small businesses, on the other hand, were seen as obstacles to economic growth because they could not effectively utilise advanced technological systems. Every effort was made to encourage industrial mergers and amalgamations, for the big fish to eat the little, so that the economic advantages of the new technology could be fully maximised. Indeed, every other aspect of society was subordinated to this overriding goal such that little consideration was given to the social implications of these economic changes. For example, the creation of boring, monotonous jobs in modern large factories was often regarded as the necessary and inevitable cost of higher economic growth.

As part and parcel of this process, priority was given to the creation of a close partnership between industry and the state so that the general planning process could operate more efficiently. Governments could ease the social and economic strains created by market forces by integrating social welfare policies with the general needs of industry. They could also fulfil a positive role in the economic rejuvenation of the country by encouraging mergers and take-overs through such agencies as the Industrial Reorganisation Corporation and later, during the 1970s, the National Enterprise Board. The main purpose of this policy was to create a technologically advanced, capital intensive economy which would be highly competitive in world markets.

Such an industrial strategy assumed the end of a self-interested capitalism characterised by class conflict and the persistence of political ideologies which, in the past, had polarised society. On the contrary, 'welfare-' or 'post-capitalism' had eroded traditional class divisions and replaced them by a set of shared values which emphasised the desirability of technological progress, economic growth and the raising of living standards. There were few ideological differences between the political parties; both Labour and Conservative were seen to be committed to the corporatist mixed economy and they only differed in the means to be employed.

By the late 1970s this industrial policy was regarded as a failure. It had not only been unable to solve the problems of the economy but also it had created a wide range of social tensions which could be seen to be the outcome of the economic and social policies of the 1960s. The British economy continued to be characterised by low productivity, non-competitiveness and outdated technology. In addition, 'structural rationalisation' had produced social problems which, arguably, were the result of urban renewal and re-housing schemes, population migration and the creation of psychologically unsatisfying work environments. Further, it was held that corporatism was corroding the core values of Western liberal-democratic society; not only were state welfare services killing incentives and the will to work, but economic planning was eroding the ability of businesses to take risks, to innovate and to capture new markets. It was claimed that British society was becoming dominated by mediocrity and bureaucratism and that the freedom of the individual was being subordinated to the state. Britain, in short, was rapidly acquiring the alleged characteristics of East European state socialist countries.

In the late 1970s, therefore, a new direction was sought. There seemed to be only two choices: either to continue to pursue the corporatist road until the East European goal had been achieved, or to bring back classical capitalism. Quite obviously, the Thatcher Conservative Government chose the latter. The state was to be cut back, economic regulations to be diluted if not abandoned, and market forces to be liberated from political interference. The bearers of this new entrepreneurial culture were to be the independent businessmen. If small-scale and family-owned businesses were viewed as inefficient and a constraint upon economic growth in the 1960s, by the late 1970s they were seen by many politicians — not exclusively within the Conservative Party — as a fundamental plank in the programme to bring about a regeneration of not only the economy, but society in general. They are, then, now regarded as the solution to a wide range of economic and social problems; as the means whereby the tensions and failures of the economic strategy of the 1960s can be corrected. This small business panacea, however, is founded upon highly questionable assumptions.

The view that small businesses create employment is based on the notion that for a given level of capital investment more work is created than in large-scale technological enterprises. But, as recent research has shown, small enterprises can be highly capital intensive in certain sectors of the economy; they are small *because* of this and, consequently, do not create jobs.[2] Further, the alleged employment attractions of small businesses disregard the lower wages, fewer fringe benefits and inferior working conditions which often prevail.[3] Perhaps it is not coincidental that these conditions are often associated with low levels of unionisation among workers in small-scale enterprises.[4] Indeed, it is possibly because of this that large corporations support the Thatcher government's small business strategy since it is often cheaper for them to 'subcontract' short-term specialist work to small-scale enterprises. The notion, then, that small businesses are autonomous sources of employment that can counter economic recession is largely a myth. On the contrary, they are often heavily dependent upon the requirements of large-scale corporations which use them according to variable market conditions.[5] In fact, as *Small Business, Big Future* states, without small firms and the self-employed, 'large business could not function effectively'.

It is also claimed that small businesses offer a solution to the problems of absenteeism, labour turnover and industrial discontent. According to the Conservative Party, 'working relationships are easier and happier in small companies. Many of the problems that arise in large enterprises are unknown in firms where the owner-manager knows and is known to all of his employees'.[6] But once again, the evidence on this is inconclusive and certainly an insufficient basis for industrial policy. Even if we assume that there is a lower incidence of management-worker conflict in smaller enterprises this probably has less to do with the effects of size *per se* than to other conditions; for example, styles of supervision and employer control.[7] In small businesses, worker commitment can be encouraged by the cultivation of personal relationships that emphasise the qualities of either egalitarianism or paternalism. With the former, employers establish close links with employees by stressing the team and co-operative nature of their enterprises. With paternalism, on the other hand, employers recognise their responsibilities for the personal welfare of their staff who, in turn, accept that employers have the *right* to tell them what to do. Whichever strategy is used the effect is likely to be much the same; the level of unionisation will be low and workers will be highly committed to the employer's goals. For many, this is an appealing proposition since most of Britain's problems are associated with manager-worker conflict. Small firms, then, are regarded as a ready-made solution to industrial strife.

Further, it is claimed that small businesses offer a cure to the problems of inner urban areas. Hence, recent Tory proposals for the creation of enterprise zones which, by diluting various statutory regulations, are intended to attract small, labour-intensive businesses in order to reverse the long-term pauperisation of the metropolitan conurbations. However, critics have argued that the real attraction of this policy is the opportunity it provides for using low-paid labour. Consequently, local small employers can take advantage of, for instance, women in unskilled and semi-skilled jobs who, because of family commitments, are often unable to travel to better-paid work. But are small employers the real beneficiaries? When they are little more than subcontractors to large-scale corporations producing short runs of specialist commodities, the real gains of enterprise zones would seem to accrue to big rather than small businesses.

In view of these remarks we are in a better position to understand the appeal for many people of the government's small business strategy. In a nutshell, it offers a solution to one of the major problems confronting industry *as diagnosed* by employers, managers and politicians; that is, *the management of labour.* If large-scale corporations have created circumstances in which unionism and working-class consciousness flourishes, small businesses are seen as a means by which this alleged 'imbalance' of power can be redressed. In addition, they offer numerous possibilities whereby a wide range of legislation enacted to improve the conditions of employees cannot be effectively enforced. There is an insufficient number of factory inspectors, health and safety officers, and so on, to guarantee that the statutory requirements in these enterprises are fully implemented.

However, the attractions of small-scale enterprises are not only economic but also symbolic and cultural. This is linked to the widely-held assumption that entrepreneurs, business owners and 'self-made' men in general, built Western capitalism. Through determination and considerable self-sacrifice they are often considered to be the founding fathers of the world's most successful economic order. Furthermore, their admirers would lead us to believe that by their efforts, the basis for free, liberal-democratic society was created. This is not only because their self-interested entrepreneurship destroyed traditional agrarian society but that they established the essential democratic rights of individuals in the 'new' society. According to popular mythology – most strongly expressed in the United States and by successful entrepreneurs themselves – capitalism provides everyone with the potential to become a capitalist. In other words, life is a race in which all start as equals; those who are prepared to work hard and make the necessary effort can 'make it' while the rest 'go to the wall'. But if everyone can be a capitalist who provides the labour? The rhetoric says little about this except that such people tend to be less 'able', 'enterprising' and 'intelligent' since otherwise they, too, would be entrepreneurs. But again the desirable qualities of Western capitalism are confirmed; while everyone is given the opportunity to become a capitalist, work and material sustenance are given to those less successful in the race. Implicitly, therefore, there has always been a strong undercurrent of thought in Western countries – especially in the United States – which claims that the low-paid are, in many ways, intellectually inferior to others. By contrast, entrepreneurs embody society's greatest virtues; they are 'enterprising' and the pioneers of economic progress. Further, they are 'generous' people; witness their much publicised acts of benevolence and charity.[8]

Such, then, is the popular image of the early entrepreneurs as it persists today. Indeed, this essentially 'romantic' view has been able to withstand the criticism that the material fortunes of the few are built upon the exploitation of the many. But to regard entrepreneurs as exploiters goes against the grain. In the folklore of the middle classes in the West, the ideological battle between nineteenth-century entrepreneurs and the twentieth-century critics has been lost – by the critics.

But where are the entrepreneurs of contemporary capitalism? Despite their romantic appeal how important are they as an economic force? Many would argue that corporatism not only in Britain but throughout the Western world has destroyed the opportunities for entrepreneurial endeavour. While 'structural rationalisation' has reinforced the domination of large-scale business corporations, the social democratic path – favoured until recently by politicians of both major political parties – has strengthened the power of the state and of organised labour. The partnership between big business, trade unions and the state for the orderly and planned development of a mixed economy would seem to have reduced the possibilities for individuals to 'make it on their own'. In a sense, this has made contemporary entrepreneurs even more appealing to many people. Witness the publicity given, for example, to Sir Freddie Laker. Could there be a better example of a 'self-made' man developing an enterprise for the benefit of the people? But while such individuals may personify the core values of Western capitalism, the inner dynamic of this selfsame system is reducing the possibilities for such personal careers.

Nevertheless, there are still individuals who, instead of acquiring educational qualifications and pursuing careers within large-scale corporations decide to 'go it alone'; in other words, to risk their own or borrowed assets in order to start business enterprises. It is in this sense that we use the term 'self-made'. But who are these people? Do they represent a distinctive psychological type who are motivated to accumulate in a rather exceptional manner? Does the taxation system affect their aspirations, motivations and attitudes towards accumulation? Do their beliefs and ways of life still reflect the core values of classical capitalism? These are questions that have to be answered, particularly when the government of an economy as significant as that of Britain formulates policies on the basis of assumptions in each of these areas. But if we are to move beyond the realm of rhetoric and assumption, it is necessary to study the *actual* attitudes and behaviour of business owners, entrepreneurs and 'self-made' men. Only then is it possible to unravel the relative mixes of myth and reality.

Notes

1. *Small Business, Big Future*, Conservative Central Office, London, p. 3.
2. For research which indicates the shortcomings of the small business sector as a sorce of job creation see, S. Fothergill and G. Gudgin, *The Job Generation Process in Britain*, Centre for Environmental Studies, Report No. 32 (London, 1979).
3. This, of course, will vary within different sectors of the economy. According to the Bolton Report, 'the lower earnings in small firms, as compared with large, must be mainly attributed to lower wage rates for similar jobs'. *Report of the Committee of Inquiry on Small Firms* (The Bolton Report), Cmnd. 4811, (London, 1971), para 2. 39.
4. See, for example, the Bolton Report, ibid., para. 2. 41.
5. A. Friedman, *Industry and Labour* (London, 1977), chap. 8. According to the *Financial Times* the interest of big business in the promotion of new small-scale enterprises can be explained by the fact that 'there are good commercial reasons, such as the increasing need to hive off peripheral activities to ex-employees or new entrepreneurs who can do them better and cheaper than the mother company' (29.3.77).
6. *Small Business, Big Future*, p. 4.
7. J. Curran and J. Stanworth, 'Worker Involvement and Social Relations in the Small Firm', *Sociological Review*, vol. 27 (1979).
8. For a summary of this whole mythology see C. Wright Mills, *White Collar* (New York, 1951).

2 SMALL BUSINESS OWNERS IN THE MODERN ECONOMY

In Britain, as in all Western countries, there is a growing concentration of industrial, commercial and financial resources. To give a few, but important, statistics, the one hundred largest manufacturing companies provide employment for roughly one-third of the labour force and account for approximately 35 per cent of net output. Although the level of concentration is lower in the service sector, approximately one-third of those employed are in enterprises with more than 500 workers. Thus, as many observers have suggested, although outright monopoly is rare, restricted competition between a few business giants is becoming increasingly common.[1]

This concentration has led to a decline in the opportunities available for the formation and growth of small owner-managed businesses. These have been dwarfed by publicly-quoted joint-stock companies where there is often a separation between legal ownership and managerial control. The functions of 'old-style' entrepreneurs are now subdivided among managers, experts and technical workers who collectively determine the nature and direction of business activities. The growing domination of large-scale corporations has consequently changed the pattern of personal occupational success. The entrepreneurial ideal has been superseded by managerial, professional and bureaucratic careers; instead of risk-taking on the basis of personal assets, success is acquired by promotion within clearly-defined organisational structures.[2]

The implications of these changes extend beyond the boundaries of industrial and commercial organisations. More specifically, they have affected the nature of the educational system which is now regarded as the backbone of the meritocratic society. If, during the nineteenth century — according to the proponents of the new capitalist order — everyone could risk their capital for the purposes of monetary gain, it is now argued that there is competition among equals within the educational system. This then determines the allocation of life chances and occupational success. Consequently, there is little apparent incentive to embark upon the hazards of entrepreneurship since secure incomes and careers are available within well-established bureaucracies. Despite these broad economic and social trends, however, not all opportunities for business formation have been completely eliminated.

Perhaps an over-emphasis upon corporatism, the state and big business has detracted attention from the continued importance of smaller, owner-managed enterprises and those individuals who risk their capital rather than embark upon more conventional career patterns. The economic contribution of these individuals has been confirmed by the Bolton Report, which discusses the circumstances and characteristics of small businesses. The owners of these tend to be entrepreneurs in the classical sense of the word in that they both risk their own capital and personally supervise the day-to-day activities of their enterprises. Although the proportion of these businesses has been declining since the 1920s, the Report emphasises their continuing importance. Thus, during the late 1960s, there were still 1¼ million small enterprises employing six million people: approximately one quarter of the total working population accounting for roughly 20 per cent of the gross national product.[3]

The search for active proprietors, then, is essentially an enquiry into the small business sector of the economy. In fact, this is emphasised by the Bolton Report which stresses the strategic significance of this sector as an outlet for enterprising and independent-minded people. The Report argues that small firms perform a 'vital role in the preservation of a competitive private enterprise system' and 'to ask whether there is a future for the small firm in the new age of giant companies, international combines and universal intervention by governments, is therefore tantamount to asking whether the future of private enterprise capitalism, as we have known it in this country is threatened'.[4]

The fact that entrepreneurs still exist does not mean they flourish everywhere. Clearly, there are fewer opportunities available for small business formation in capital-intensive industries. By definition, the creation of enterprises in these areas normally requires a heavy initial outlay for plant, equipment and stock. The petrochemical, automobile and advanced technological sectors, for example, are hardly conducive to the formation of new small-scale enterprises.[5] The corporate giants have these sewn up; only the state can offer any kind of challenge to their monopoly dominance. Nevertheless, it is possible to identify four areas in the manufacturing sector where entrepreneurs and privately-owned small businesses are likely to be found,

First . . . in such traditional industries as cotton, wool, hosiery and footwear, and also printing and publishing. Second . . . the engineering and metal-working industries, often providing or sub-contracting services to larger concerns – the specialist servants or myriad small dependents of major industries. Third . . . those sectors which have long favoured the small entrepreneur: consumer goods trades with low costs and high labour content, products with strong elements of fashion and specialisation, like furniture and clothing. Finally . . . a new generation of small firms in such areas as plastics, scientific instruments and electronics.[6]

In other words, the circumstances favourable to the establishment and growth of small businesses in manufacturing are *labour intensiveness, subcontracting* in the production of specialist goods and services, *small-scale technological innovation*, and *market variability*. These factors provide the opportunity for those with a minimum of capital to start their own small-scale enterprises. Of these, labour intensiveness is probably the most important; so long as the starting of a business requires the use of labour rather than capital assets, there are possibilities for 'self-made' men.

However, it could be said that a large part of manufacturing industry has become more capital intensive and this has restricted the entry of new, small-scale businesses. Consequently, although some opportunities remain in manufacturing, the real possibilities for entrepreneurship are within the personal services sector of the economy where, as Table 1 illustrates, the incidence of small firms is relatively high.

The opportunities offered by the personal services sector are also confirmed by recent employment data. In 1971, for example, the self-employed and those who ran their own businesses and employed others represented only 1.5 per cent of the occupied population in manufacturing industry. By contrast, the proportions in construction (26 per cent), the distributive trades (18 per cent) and 'miscellaneous services' (19 per cent) were considerably higher. Furthermore, in certain personal services – those provided by builders, shopkeepers, lawyers, dentists, chiropodists, publicans, hoteliers, shoe repairers and watch repairers – employers and the self-employed actually *outnumbered* employees.[7] If, then, nineteenth-century entrepreneurs were essentially manufacturers, their latter-day counterparts are providers of services. As such they are not simply relics of the past but the product of newly created structural changes which have brought about a rapid expansion of personal services. It is within this sector that less initial capital is required. During the early stages of business growth, for instance, the only assets may consist of the proprietor's own labour, unpaid family assistance and the use of domestic items such as the telephone, car and

Table 1: Proportion of Small Firms in Selected Industries

Industrial Group	Small firms as percentage of all firms		
	Nos employed	Net output	No. of firms
Personal services sector			
Hotels & catering	75	73	96
Retail trades	49	32	96
Road transport	36	26	85
Building & construction	33	27	92
Motor trades	32	29	87
Wholesale trades	25	11	77
Miscellaneous services	82	68	99
Manufacturing	20	16	94
Mining/Quarrying	20	20	77
Total: All groups	31	21	93

Source:
Bolton Report p. 33 (Table 3.1).
Note:
The statistical definition of 'small firm' adopted by the Bolton Committee varies according to industrial group. They are as follows: manufacturing (200 employees or less); retail trades (turnover £50,000 p.a. or less); construction (25 employees or less); wholesale trades (turnover £200,000 p.a. or less); mining/quarrying (25 employees or less); motor trades (turnover £100,000 p.a. or less); miscellaneous services (turnover £50,000 p.a. or less); road transport (5 vehicles or less); hotels and catering (all, excluding multiples and brewery-managed public houses).

house. It is only at a later stage, when the business has become fairly well established, that the proprietor may decide to hire regular labour and acquire premises that are separate from the home. In fact, early decisions of this sort are probably the most crucial in the careers of many 'self-made' men.

According to the Wilson Report the personal services sector covers wholesaling, retailing, hotels, catering, construction and building, motor trades, road haulage and professional services.[8] Despite this diversity, they all share a number of characteristics which encourage the formation of business enterprises. First, they tend to be labour intensive. Secondly, markets are variable with demand, preference and fashion continuously changing. Thirdly, the very large number of small-scale enterprises makes it difficult for statutory requirements, which normally constrain the activities of large-scale manufacturing establishments, to be effectively enforced. Finally, the widespread use of *real* money is conducive to the operation of an 'informal' or 'black' economy in which individuals may experiment 'on their own' in their spare time and, possibly, during periods when they are unemployed.[9] This enables them to test the market, acquire rudimentary business skills and to accumulate a small amount of capital which can then be used for the purposes of setting up a full-time business. According to some observers, the 'black' economy is a problem if only because of the tax revenue which is lost to the state. Nevertheless, it does fulfil a useful function in training many future entrepreneurs and business owners. Indeed, the structure and operation of the personal services sector are such that they are always likely to provide possibilities for the creation of small businesses. It is difficult to envisage circumstances whereby even the greatest extension of state activity and the ever-increasing influence of big corporations could completely seal off such opportunities. If, then, we ask the question, 'Where are small business owners likely to be found?' the answer is within the personal services sector.

But, as stated at the end of the last chapter, if we are to separate myth from reality it is necessary not only to talk *about* business owners but also to talk *with* them. The rest of this book, therefore, is devoted to the ways in which a number of entrepreneurs describe their own experiences — both personal and business — as well as the world in which they live. In order to collect such accounts we interviewed the proprietors of a range of businesses in the personal services sector during the autumn of 1979. At one extreme were the self-employed and at the other, a company with 1,000 employees and an annual turnover of £20 million. Thus, we talked with proprietors at different stages of business growth; in other words, some were more successful than others. While there were those who had chosen to consolidate and to 'sit' on their assets, others were committed to making money in a big way. Consequently, we found it necessary to differentiate between the owners of four distinct types of business enterprise — the *'self-employed'*, *'small employers'*, *'owner-controllers'*, and *'owner-directors'*. The classification is based upon the work role of the business owner because it is a useful index of the nature of his enterprise as it will tend to *reflect*, for example, size of labour force and level of trading. It therefore has a general applicability which any single quantitative measure, such as number of employees, lacks. Thus, the four types of employer may be defined as follows,

The *self-employed* who work for themselves and formally employ no labour. However, they are often dependent upon the unpaid services of family members, particularly their wives.
Small employers who work alongside their workers but, in addition, undertake the administrative and managerial tasks of running their

own businesses.

Owner-controllers who do not work alongside their employees but, instead, are *solely* and *singularly* responsible for the administration and management of their businesses.

Owner-directors who control enterprises with developed managerial hierarchies so that administrative tasks are subdivided and delegated to executive directors and other senior personnel.[10]

In all we talked with 96 active proprietors; of these 25 were self-employed, 29 were small employers, 26 were owner-controllers and 16 were owner-directors. In addition, we met twelve senior managers employed by owner-directors in order to understand more fully how these proprietors ran their businesses. Thus, we interviewed 108 people from 87 separate enterprises. The number of proprietors is greater than the number of businesses simply because some of these were joint ventures. Of the 96 active proprietors, 72 had founded their businesses while the remaining 24 had inherited them, normally from their fathers. All of the 'inheritors' had been responsible for expanding, often in a dramatic fashion, the enterprises which they had taken over. If, then, they had not confronted the difficulties of starting a business they had been pre-occupied with the problems of business growth.

In order to establish contact in the personal services sector we began our investigation by interviewing those who were running enterprises in the building industry. We did so for a number of reasons. In the first place, it is probably the easiest branch of the economy in which technically less qualified employees can start a business. Indeed, the industry is characterised by a strong tradition of 'self-made' men, of people who start with virtually no assets but die as multi-millionaires and leave large, well-established companies.[11] Because so few initial capital assets are required a worker can 'experiment' in his spare time and, on the basis of this, decide whether or not to run a business. He can, for example, use his own house as premises and his car and other domestic possessions for the purposes of the business. It is only at a later stage that he needs to decide whether to become an employer of labour rather than remaining as self-employed. In fact, a number of the largest companies in the industry started in this way. Further, the building industry embodies many of the essential features of the personal services sector of the economy as outlined above. For instance, not only is it labour intensive but enterprises are confronted with a variable market. It is also difficult for statutory bodies to supervise the activities of those smaller businesses which often deal directly with the public at large in *real* money. The building industry, then, is typical of the 'non-professional' personal services sector in that it is possible for someone lacking in formal 'meritocratic' qualifications and with a minimum of capital, to create and expand a business. Finally, as part and parcel of business expansion there is often a tendency for a diversification of interests to occur; this tends to be almost entirely within the personal services rather than in the manufacturing sector of the economy. We found it was quite common for building firms to diversify not only into those areas closely associated with the industry such as, for example, estate agencies, property management, plant and tool hire, but also into antique shops, restaurants, garden centres, hotels, garages, electrical stores, vehicle hire and insurance brokerages. Such activities are not only perceived as investment propositions but as means whereby cash flows can be improved. We have, then, taken the opportunity of selecting those businesses whose interests do not lie exclusively within the building industry; indeed, they represent a range of activities within the personal services sector in general. In addition, however, we talked to proprietors who had no associations with the building industry. These included business owners in various areas of the distributive, retail and catering trades; for example, restauranteurs, garage proprietors, shopkeepers and road haulage contractors.

Our method for collecting the information was quite simple. We wrote to a number of enterprises selected from trade registers and the lists of various employers' associations. The overwhelming majority said they would be willing to co-operate in the study. From these, we chose businesses which were representative of the *four categories* outlined above. After making contact with the proprietors of these we had lengthy meetings lasting anything from between one and six hours. These sessions were conducted between August and November 1979, recorded on tape and later transcribed. In this book we present quotations derived from the interviews. The number and distribution of these, in terms of their selection from our four categories of proprietor, are listed in Table 2.

From Table 2 it can be seen that we use 242 quotations. These are taken from 17 self-employed men, 22 small employers, 20 owner-controllers, 15 owner-directors and 9 of their senior managers. In all, the quotations are selected from 83 of the 108 people we interviewed. Thus, the range of owners cited and the quotations used in the text are fairly well spread, although rather more are drawn from owner-director enterprises since we interviewed senior managers as well as the active proprietors.

Table 2: The Number and Distribution of Quotations

Category	No. of enterprises	No. of owners (no. of founders in parenthesis)	No. of owners cited in text	No. of quotes from owners	No. of senior managers	No. of senior managers cited in text	No. of quotes from senior managers	Total no. of quotes cited
Self-employed	25	25 (25)	17	36	–	–	–	36
Small employers	25	29 (27)	22	65	–	–	–	65
Owner-contollers	24	26 (15)	20	54	–	–	–	54
Owner-directors	13	16 (5)	15	56	12	9	31	87
Total	87	96 (72)	74	211	12	9	31	242

In the text we have given fictional names to those respondents who are cited more frequently than others. This should make the book easier to read and enable various 'personalities' to appear. We take this approach one stage further in Chapter 9 when, in order to show how personal experiences shape general attitudes, we focus upon five of the people we interviewed. The quotations included in these portraits are not included in the above calculations.

Notes

1. The increasing level of industrial, financial and commercial concentration in the British economy is documented in J. Westergaard and H. Resler, *Class in a Capitalist Society* (London, 1975); and in the *Royal Commission on the Distribution of Income and Wealth, Report No. 1* (London, 1975).

2. A detailed comparison of entrepreneurial and bureaucratic careers can be found in R. Bendix, *Work and Authority in Industry* (New York, 1956).

3. *Report of the Committee of Inquiry on Small Firms*, Cmnd. 4811, (London, 1971), p. xix.

4. Ibid.

5. M.A. Utton, *Industrial Concentration* (Harmondsworth, 1970), p. 75.

6. J. Boswell, *The Rise and Decline of Small Firms* (London, 1973), p. 17.

7. R.K. Brown, 'Work' in P. Abrams (ed.), *Work, Urbanism and Inequality* (London, 1978), p. 83.

8. Committee to Review the Functioning of Financial Institutions, *The Financing of Small Firms*, Cmnd. 7503 (London, 1979), p. 54.

9. The significance of the 'informal' economy is discussed in J. Gershuny, *After Industrial Society? The Emerging Self-Service Economy* (London, 1978).

10. These categories are discussed in greater detail in our forthcoming, *The Entrepreneurial Middle Class*.

11. As witnessed by the large number of biographies that have been written on successful 'self-made' men in the industry. See, for example, A. Jenkins, *On Site 1921-71* (London, 1971). This is an account of the growth of the construction company, Taylor Woodrow.

3 PEOPLE WHO START THEIR OWN BUSINESSES

Our recurring image of entrepreneurship owes much to the efforts of historians, sociologists and psychologists. Their work suggests a model of the typical entrepreneur which colours much contemporary debate. Yet how far is their picture any more accurate than the popular image that we have already questioned? At their worst these accounts deal only in a sophisticated form of romance and rhetoric, particularly those which describe the 'captains of industry' in the era of classical capitalism. One historian, for example, has characterised them as 'busy', 'tireless' and 'profit-seeking'. Furthermore, entrepreneurial types are seen to

> . . . display a high awareness of future possibilities; they are non-conservative in the sense of having a particular interest in novelty and innovation; they possess more than average energy; and they . . . strive for the satisfaction of success or achievement.[1]

The picture of the entrepreneur who deliberately sets out to achieve maximum profit, by means of rational calculation, has received support from psychologists. An American psychologist, McClelland, has claimed that what humans do can be interpreted as an attempt to satisfy certain basic, psychological 'needs'.[2] These include those of friendship, independence, order and achievement. How such 'needs' combine in individuals tells us something about their personality and motivations. McClelland claims that entrepreneurs are marked by their exceptional drive to achieve to the extent that they are prepared to take risks, make decisions, innovate and, of course, expend considerable amounts of 'energy'. Some psychologists might stop here, but it is to McClelland's credit that he tries to establish the source of these personality characteristics, primarily by reference to parental influence during childhood. He goes on to suggest, in fact, that the Methodist revival during the Industrial Revolution in Britain was conducive to child-rearing patterns which inculcated the 'achievement motivation'.

Whether or not this argument is accepted, it at least attempts to link purely psychological features with broader social patterns. This is the domain of sociologists who have suggested that entrepreneurs may be more likely to emerge from those groups in society which are 'deprived' or 'marginal'.[3] By this they mean groups which are discriminated against, persecuted, 'looked down upon' or exceptionally exploited. This can lead individuals within such groups to experience a severe discrepancy between their *personal* attributes and the *social* role which is accorded them. Hence, for example, the 'marginality' of the black professional in a white society. The responses to marginality are varied, but it is often the case that people who are marginal may 'opt out' by setting up a business. Such an argument has often been used to explain, for example, the business success of Asians in East Africa and of East African Asians in some European countries. It may be the indignity of the 'rags' which encourages *some* individuals to pursue the 'riches' of monetary success in an extremely single-minded way. Indeed, no personal sacrifice is too great in the attainment of this goal.

This brings the argument back once again to the idea of achievement and the vigour of the entrepreneurial type which roams the pages of historical and psychological accounts. How does this 'textbook type' compare with the individuals who co-operated in our interview study? According to academic analysis it should be possible to predict those who are likely to start their own businesses and develop them into flourishing commercial enterprises. The interviews, however, suggested this is not possible; there is no clearly identifiable pattern and furthermore, the motives for starting businesses are remarkably diverse.[4]

In the interviews there was a discrepancy between *general* notions about who starts businesses and the detailed accounts of their own *personal* histories. Although many subscribe to conventional notions about 'self-made' men, a totally different set of interpretations emerges in accounts of their own and other peoples' *concrete* experiences.

In our general conversations about the psychology of the businessman, the same essential qualities are repeatedly emphasised. The owner-director of a company with fifty employees, for example, stressed the ability to ' ... wrestle with any problem that comes along and to sort it out and to never give up. There's a certain will and determination to see the thing through – and to fight all the way.' This is coupled with the qualities of *drive* and *ambition*. One of the small employers claimed that,

You've got to be a bit more *ambitious* than your immediate counterparts. For a worker to set up on his own he has got to have a little more *ambition* than the worker on either side of him who's quite happy to plod. There are a lot of problems, a lot of worries, as you go up and you've got to be able to just shrug them off I think.

There's no way that you can get worried and fussed about it. You've at least got to believe that you can succeed. I'm an incurable optimist and I believe that my big chance is just round the corner. It's been there for the last 16 years.

This opinion was echoed by Derek Bateman, a self-employed man who, in describing his working life, said,

The most important quality that I've had to call upon myself has been my *resilience* and my *determination*. I think that just about covers everything for me. My *determination* makes me work hard when I'm tired. My *resilience* helps me to recover when I've had a terrible shock, when things have gone wrong.

But for Bateman there was one further necessary quality – *independence*. As he told us, 'self-made' men are those who ' . . . have some *independence*, and who feel some *independence*. People who prefer to do things for themselves.' This quality was strongly emphasised by an owner-director who argued that starting a business,

. . . attracts people who want to be their own boss, and for that reason often go ahead, and who have got a fair amount of *initiative* and who like to be *independent*. You don't get what I call the 'safety-first' type of chap, who goes into public service. It does tend to attract the type of chap who's got what I call sturdy *independence*.

But still these assumed psychological qualities do not complete the picture. Further capacities are emphasised; more specifically, reserves of *energy* and *enthusiasm* are regarded as particularly important. According to an owner-director, with an annual turnover of £6 million, 'It's got a lot to do with the amount of *energy* one's prepared to put into it. You put the *energy* in the right direction and I think that the results are there.' In other words, you've got to be *keen*. This, for self-employed Stan Holmes, was very important,

A fellow has got to have ambition, he's got to be *keen* and he's got to be a person who's got to be *keen* all the time, seven days a week and not just one day a week. I can't relax. I've got a *keenness* in my work. Birds are my relaxation. You've got to have relaxation but you've still got to be *keen* every day. I'm as *keen* today when I walk out of that door at 7.30 in the morning as I was 17 years ago and that's being honest about it. Because if I wasn't I wouldn't be where I am today. I'm not being big-headed about it. Everybody can't be that *keen*, therefore it's not everybody that could run a business.

But energy has to be channelled in the right direction; it requires *self-discipline* to ensure that total priority is given to work and that business will always come before pleasure.

These, then, are the assumed qualities necessary to be a businessman. They appear as much in the entrepreneurial manuals of the early nineteenth century, as in the autobiographies of contemporary 'self-made' men such that they have become part and parcel of conventional wisdom. Furthermore, these are generally seen as 'inborn' and genetically determined qualities. The personality is not considered to be subject to social modification; either an individual has got it or he hasn't! This opinion was clearly reflected in the attitudes of Keith Large, an owner-controller with approximately 35 workers,

Let's face it, what are we? We're just an intelligent bloody animal aren't we? It's the survival of the fittest. And all animals have hierarchy — it's just the way it's got to be. Everybody can't be equal. I accept there may be people above me. As I was explaining to my children the other day, some people are just born gifted — and this applies to business too.

But even so, the successful businessman must also have a number of social skills, especially the capacity for hard work and the ability to take risks. For Barry Small, a small employer with four employees, the explanation for business success was very simple: 'It's usually somebody that's not afraid of work; it's graft, hard work and that is the way to be successful.'

For Keith Large, it was not enough to be gifted. You have, '... to work bloody hard to develop the gift. You may have the opportunity. You may have the luck. Unless you work bloody hard at it you've never going to develop it.'

But you must also be able to take risks which, according to many respondents, people are now less prepared to do. As the wife of self-employed Norman Brown claimed,

You've got to be the sort of person who's prepared to take a bit of a risk, and take the responsibility. A lot of people would never want it. They would rather have a job where they are told what to do — they do it and then at the end of the week they get their wages. That's the sort of job they want.

The motivation underlying the hard work and the risk that the 'self-made' man is prepared to take is seen by many as monetary gain. Comments emphasising the cash rewards of entrepreneurial risk were repeated many times, one of the more explicit being put forward by the owner-controller of a company with a £100,000 turnover. He stated, 'I always think I'm going to make a fortune, and the day I stop thinking about it, I shall be lost.' Similarly, self-employed Mel Morgan emphasised that people who run their own businesses,

> . . . get to the till and see the pound note sign and then it gets bigger and bigger until it completely fills their eyes — and that's all it is. They get more money if they work for themselves — the more they do, the more they are going to get.

It seems, then, that business owners have a particularly distinctive attitude of mind which emphasises a commitment to profit-making for *its own sake*. Personal satisfaction is acquired through developing a business rather than by enjoying a high personal standard of living. This is the picture of the business proprietor as conveyed by the interviews and it contains few surprises. He is seen to be hard-working, ambitious, energetic and motivated by economic gain. This image has persisted over the decades, despite the dramatic changes which have occurred both within the economy and in the nature of business enterprises. Yet the whole picture is distorted by two fundamental flaws. First, ambitious, hard-working and energetic people are to be found in all walks of life and not solely among business proprietors. These notions, then, do not enable us to identify a distinguishable entrepreneurial type. Secondly, the image ignores a number of other important factors which are crucial in accounting for the *concrete* experiences of the people we interviewed.

When we turned from asking questions about the necessary personal qualities needed for business success *in general* to specific accounts of how they *actually* started their own enterprises, very different explanations were put forward. These were factual accounts within which there was no place for 'conventional wisdom' and received, everyday rhetoric. Analysis of these accounts indicates that many proprietors are motivated by a wide range of social and non-economic factors of the sort that are often neglected in general discussions of entrepreneurial types. Thus, business formation and growth is often not the outcome of exceptional personal capacities of *drive, determination* and *ambition* but a function of various forms of personal discontent and random occurrence. Hence, for many of the people we interviewed, the reason for starting a business was not out of a desire ultimately to become a successful entrepreneur, but as a *rejection* of working for somebody else. In other words, setting up a business – which often meant becoming self-employed in the first instance – was the result of a conscious decision to 'drop out'. But, of course, to 'drop out' can be a variable experience. Some had merely wished to reject their previous employee status, while others aimed to 'opt out' of society altogether. There are, then, different degrees of resentment for which going into business offers some kind of solution. In rejecting the employee role, two major factors are emphasised – authority and the wage/profit relationship. Thus, for some, starting a business represents an escape from the control of others.[5] As an owner-controller with a turnover of £250,000 told us, 'I'm one of those people who find it very difficult to work under other people if I'm truthful. It's not something I do very well, put it that way. And that, amongst other things, is what made me start on my own.' Similarly, a self-employed man recalled, 'I was sort of an independent nature. Although I always got on alright working for people I was never particularly happy when I wasn't in charge of my own destiny.' These attitudes, then, could lead to tensions which were the reason for them 'going it alone'. As one small employer had told his last boss, 'Poke the job up your arse – I'm going on my own.'

But there were others who felt that, as employees, they were being exploited. As Mel Morgan recalled, 'I decided I was fed up with other people getting the money that I was really earning for them. They were all running about in fast cars and I was getting nothing.' To this we can add another self-employed man's considered opinion that, 'Any employer is a greedy bugger isn't he? He thinks he can earn more than by working for somebody else.' An employee who thinks in these terms has some notion of the profit margins to be made by an employer from the work produced by his employees. Economic calculation of this sort is likely to produce either a socialist or a new capitalist!

But starting a business is also seen as an escape from society in general; in other words, as a means of 'dropping out' completely. Norman Brown and his wife Mary had jointly decided that setting up a business was the only way to cope with the pressures of contemporary living and although he was running a small but successful business, further growth was not their intention. Quite the reverse in fact. As Mary Brown told us,

> Norman could earn a lot more by working much longer hours but we chose to work less hours and have more free time. Therefore, we have a lower *material* standard of living but it suits us better ... there's too much emphasis on materialism, material values. The Conservatives say they're the party of the small businessman but what they're driving at isn't what we're driving at. They're seeing it very much again in terms of materialism. They would immediately assume anyone who sets up in business wants to expand. They would never think of it in terms of setting up a business and staying the same size.

To this Norman added,

> Where else can you have the freedom to say 'Well, I'm not getting up today at seven o'clock.' If the wife says to me, 'Well I'm off to take the kids to the beach.' How else can you, in my way of living, with my income, have a lot to say about where and when you work?

This sense of freedom and autonomy was frequently mentioned by owners of the smaller businesses despite the fact that they are rarely able to exercise the options open to them. The mere fact that it is possible is enough. To give but one of many illustrations of this, a self-employed proprietor said,

> Working for yourself you can always take it easy. Have a day at the races or something. You've always got it in the back of your mind that you can't get the sack for a start. Even though you never do, you could lay in bed until midday and no one is going to tick you off.

But beyond a certain size the pressures of running a business soon curb this apparent freedom. Indeed, only the owners of the largest enterprises, where ownership and control could be effectively separated, are able to enjoy this autonomy. Many of the self-employed and the smaller employers that we talked to were, in fact, very uneasy about further expansion because of the effect on their personal freedom and their capacity to 'opt out'. For these people starting a business is often an explicit *rejection* of the capitalist ethic and any subsequent business growth is an almost accidental part of a dynamic over which they often feel they have very little control. A person starts on his own, business builds up, and extra staff have to be employed. The proprietor then finds that he *has* to adapt himself to the responsibilities of being an employer and give up his autonomy. Such processes are rarely considered in accounts of entrepreneurial behaviour.

If starting a business enables a person to escape from the constraints of authority, the wage-profit relationship and other features of being an employee, it also allows him to 'do a good job'. This was another factor in Norman Brown's decision to 'go it alone'. 'I got fed up with being told how to do things which I knew were wrong. I had the manual skill and the technical ability to go on my own. That's the only way you can do what you want to do − to be on your own.' Brown's statement was confirmed by a small employer who said, 'When I'm doing a job it's my decision and freedom as to whether I do it one way or another. Rather than worry about what some other chap wants me to do.' As employees, these men had felt they were unable to exercise their skills and they 'opted out' in order to produce good quality work. Such sentiments often persist long after the formation of a business. Although many of the people that we interviewed were motivated by economic gain, this was often bounded by the desire to produce 'a good job', 'something that is useful', 'something that the customer will be pleased with'. Peter Rivard, a well-established small employer with eight workers, summed it up as follows,

> The only thing is the satisfaction that you're doing a decent job otherwise you wouldn't keep the custom. You know you're doing a good turn to the people who need you. You've got to work hard yourself to be fair to the customer. You see, if I run about in a car all day long it's got to go on their bill and up goes the cost.

Although such opinions are expressed by a minority, it is interesting that these small employers see themselves primarily as tradesmen and artisans rather than businessmen. Much of the rhetoric surrounding entrepreneurs tends to forget this.

Though starting a business is often a conscious decision to escape the employee role, there are a number of factors which sometimes force people into this commitment. For instance, the chance circumstances of redundancy, unemployment or industrial injury often provide the trigger. Redundancy payments especially among middle-class,

salaried professionals can provide just enough working capital for them
to set up as consultants and industrial advisers, to escape from the 'rat
race' by buying small-holdings in the West of England, or to buy pubs,
restaurants and shops in the personal services sector. Among those in
our own study, Derek Bateman had used his redundancy payment to
start his own business: 'I worked for a shipping firm and redundancy
came and so I decided that I'd do one of two things. I'd take the redundancy and get a pub or – as building was booming at the time – I
became a jobbing builder.' Another self-employed proprietor, however,
had not been quite so fortunate. As he explained,

> The bloke I was working for got short of work and so he had to
> stand me off. So I had to find my own work. So more or less, I was
> pushed into it. It's a big step to take when you have had a good job.
> I started off with the dole and then got contacts working locally.
> And so I started off penniless.

Though this proprietor had received no redundancy pay, he had his
skills so he could undertake small jobs and become established with a
regular circle of customers. Although unemployment benefit may not
be intended as venture capital for new businesses, in many sectors of
the economy – especially within the personal services – it can be a
crucial part of the dynamic!

Occasionally loss of work, through industrial accident or sickness,
persuades people to start their own businesses. For instance, the co-
proprietor of a small business recounted the origins of his own enterprise in the following manner,

> I was in engineering. I worked as a fitter for about 18 months and
> they said that I was allergic to metal so they advised me to pack up
> work. Then I was quite lucky. I saw an old friend of mine, we hap-
> pened to be having a drink, and he just said, 'How are you doing?'
> And I said, 'Well I don't know – I'm supposed to pack up what I'm
> doing.' So he said, 'You come and join me if you want to.' And
> that's how I started, I didn't intend to start on my own. I'd got no
> idea because I was always contented in the engineering work.

Sheer luck is sometimes an important element as Ray Nichols, an
owner-controller with 20 workers and an annual turnover of £1¼
million, told us,

One day, in 1948, I was on my bike and I came along the back roads and there was a chap on a lawn sawing away. Blimey, I thought, old Bill Cannon. I gave him a whistle and he said, 'What are you doing?' I said, 'I'm out of the army and I've got a fortnight's holiday.' He said, 'I've got a nice lot of work on, you come and work for me.' And so I started and I didn't get my holiday for six years. And then in about 1958 he persuaded me to take a more active managerial role. I didn't really want it. And then when he died he left a letter saying that he wanted me to take over the business. And so I've built it up since then.

It was, then, only by chance that he found himself being offered a job and then later, the business. Others also referred to 'luck' as the major explanation for what they were now doing. To give but two examples, Keith Large claimed,

I've had people say to me, 'Christ, I'd never have thought you'd have gone into business on your own.' I think a lot of it, rather than being the right person, is being in the right place at the right time. Speaking personally, I think if the opportunity hadn't arisen, I'd still be wielding a hammer with the rest of them.

Dick Crook, a small employer also remarked, 'My whole life has been a series of coincidences, accidents or whatever you like to call them, which have pushed me in certain directions.'

These various examples do not deny that many businesses are set up with determinedly money-making motives but they do challenge the notion that every aspiring 'self-made' man glows with entrepreneurial fervour. It seems to us that the conventional view of the entrepreneurial type has serious shortcomings. It gives insufficient attention to the highly variable non-monetary factors that are often central to the formation of business enterprises and it imposes 'rational' and 'logical' explanations upon experiences and behaviour that are extremely diverse, personal and random. It is virtually impossible to predict those who will become entrepreneurs, business proprietors and 'self-made' men and yet the conventional wisdom persists. Indeed, even the people we interviewed subscribe to these general notions although they account for their own personal and concrete experiences in a very different fashion. We suspect that the persistence of this well-established belief in an entrepreneurial type performs an important function in present-day society. It reasserts the supremacy of 'individualism', 'personal achievement', 'hard work' and 'self-sacrifice' as the core principles around which Western liberal democratic society is organised. It reaffirms the force of the individual over that of society. The symbolic image of the 'self-made' man, then, is as important as his functional contribution to the economy. This, in itself, is not necessarily harmful but it makes for questionable public debate. As we noted earlier, the image of the 'self-made' man has tremendous cultural appeal as a force for regeneration in Western society. But economic policies founded upon these beliefs may prove to be less successful than is currently expected. These policies, further, assume that entrepreneurship and the incentives for business formation and growth are closely related to the operation of the tax system. It is, then, to a consideration of these issues that we now turn.

Notes

1. M. Flinn, *Origins of the Industrial Revolution* (London, 1966), p. 81.

2. D. McClelland, *The Achieving Society* (Princeton, New Jersey), 1961.

3. For a discussion of the 'marginality thesis' see, J. Stanworth and J. Curran, *Management Motivation in the Smaller Business* (Epping, 1973).

4. See, for example, the study conducted by T. Faulkner at Trent Polytechnic Small Business Centre reported in 'No Common Denominator . . . ', *Guardian* (1 February 1980).

5. This is compatible with the findings of Bechhofer and his associates in their study of small shopkeepers in Edinburgh. See, for example, F. Bechhofer, B. B. Elliot, M. Rushforth and R. Bland, 'The Petits Bourgeois in the Class Structure: the Case of the Small Shopkeepers' in F. Parkin (ed.), *The Social Analysis of Class Structure* (London, 1974). See also the results of studies summarised in the Bolton Report, pp. 23-4.

4 TAXATION, PERSONAL INCENTIVE AND BUSINESS GROWTH

There is a widely-held belief that there is a close relationship between levels of taxation and economic motivation. It is often suggested that high personal taxation in Britain has dramatically reduced business-men's propensity to save, re-invest and generally to devote energy to the expansion of their enterprises. It is one of the reasons, so it is claimed, that Britain's economic performance — by international standards — has been so disappointing. With this diagnosis in mind the Thatcher Government has proclaimed the virtues of the free market and the need for a 'new direction' in which entrepreneurial talent will be more adequately rewarded. Central to this strategy is the notion that cuts in direct taxation will provide a major incentive. As far as business owners are concerned, it is hoped that tax reductions will encourage them to re-invest and to expand within a newly-found competitive cli-mate which, in turn, will also foster the formation of new enterprises. However, despite the popular appeal of this policy, there may be a crucial flaw in the underlying assumption. No research has been able to prove conclusively that entrepreneurs are less likely to expand their businesses and to work hard because of high taxation. Given that tax cuts are such an important plank in Conservative policy, it is remark-able how few studies have been undertaken especially in the small busi-ness sector where, as we have seen, most 'self-made' men are to be found. In its pamphlet, *Small Business, Big Future*, the Conservative Party gives income tax reductions 'first priority' in the belief that 'penal rates . . . inhibit personal savings and the building up of capital neces-sary to start a business'. It also claims that it 'has rarely been as diffi-cult to start or expand a business, or to hand it on to one's children as a going concern'. This is said to be the result of capital transfer and capital gains taxes which not only prevent the handing down of wealth from one generation to the next, but also inhibit the growth of busi-nesses to their 'optimum' size. Consequently, the Conservative Party is firmly committed to reductions in these taxes and to the introduc-tion of special relief for businesses passed on within the family. Yet how far have the assumptions underlying these policies been rigorously tested?

In its study of small firms, the Bolton Committee claims that, 'in the mind of the average small businessman . . . high taxation ranks as the most important single factor in the inhibition of enterprise and the decline of the small firm sector'.[1] According to the Report, high taxes serve to reduce incentive and the ability of individuals to accumulate capital by founding, maintaining and expanding their own businesses. Consequently, a tax policy is needed which will 'restore initiative, encourage entrepreneurial activity and improve the liquidity position of small businesses'.[2] Cuts in tax on personal incomes and estates are considered 'most likely to achieve this result'. However, in a similar fashion to the Conservative Party, the Bolton Committee emphasises this more as an act of faith than as a result of firm, tangible evidence. As they admit, the effects of taxation 'are extremely hard to demonstrate and quantify' and consequently 'the disincentive effect of high taxation is exceedingly complex and controversial. It has never been convincingly demonstrated that effort and risk-taking in business respond inversely to tax changes'.[3]

Perhaps the most determined assault on all forms of state intervention for the purposes of encouraging business growth is embodied in proposals by the Conservative Minister, Sir Geoffrey Howe, for the establishment of enterprise zones. These would provide an environment within which businesses could flourish without the full force of various regulations and controls. Thus, beyond basic health, safety and environmental standards, detailed planning controls would not apply. Business owners who take the opportunity of establishing themselves in these zones would be exempt from development land tax, employment protection legislation and local rates. In addition, assurances would be given that any changes in tax law, price control and pay policy would not apply. Finally, public authorities would be compelled to dispose of land to private bidders by auction in an 'open market'. Once disposed of, such property would be entirely free from rent control. These, then, are the conditions by which Sir Geoffrey Howe would 'set about the sensible de-regulation of our economy'.[4]

Even if such a scheme is fully implemented it is unlikely from the findings of our study that it will have much effect on entrepreneurship. We found little evidence to suggest that personal taxation affects the entrepreneurial activities of business owners. Generally speaking, taxation and government controls are seen as a set of givens which operate throughout the market. In this sense, taxes are regarded as a condition of business activity to be treated in a similar manner as competitors, suppliers, creditors, employees, and so on.

In exploring the impact of personal taxation, it is necessary to distinguish between individuals *wishing to set up* in business and the viability of enterprises *already* in existence. With the former, it may be justifiably claimed that high levels of personal taxation actually encourage rather than restrict the creation of business enterprises. Employees will often refuse to work overtime because of the higher level of tax and, instead, 'moonlight' in their spare time as part of the 'black economy'. This 'hidden economy' which, it is claimed, is increasing in significance not only in Britain but in other European countries, is alleged to be a problem by some economic observers but it is an important basis for the formation of business enterprises. By undertaking work for clients in the evenings and at weekends, workers can often acquire a number of assets and skills necessary for forming a business; a network of regular customers, the cultivation of links with merchants and the suppliers of various materials, as well as the general acquisition of business and marketing abilities. As a small employer with 20 workers explained,

> A lot of people go through what we call the 'scratching' phase. They go out night times and they earn themselves a bit. And I think this is basically how it starts. I started by doing this type of work. You see, you don't pay tax that way like you do when you're doing overtime.

Similarly, an owner-controller with assets of more than £¾ million stated,

> I was running an estate on the maintenance side but during this time I was also working for myself in the evenings and at weekends. I was building up quite a substantial number of private customers so I eventually decided to go one hundred per cent on my own.

Of course it could be argued that these practices are more likely to develop in the building industry because of the skills of workers and the nature of the tasks undertaken. Craftsmen possess skills which employers cannot easily control; there is always the need for houses to be painted and decorated, burst pipes to be repaired and electrical wiring to be replaced. But, of course, there are comparable possibilities in the provision of other personal services. Hairdressers, car mechanics, solicitors and accountants, to name but a few, can all undertake private services in their spare time rather than working longer hours for their employers. In this way, they will probably pay little or no tax and, at the same time, develop the abilities necessary to start their own businesses. As Howard Crompton, the owner-director of a company with 150 employees said,

> If we got more of the money we earnt in our pockets it would be an incentive for people who want to work hard and earn money. You wouldn't get this moonlighting and such like. You get it in all sorts of trades, motor business, watchmaking, anything you like. You name it — doctors, solicitors — they all do things on the side. And I'm sure a lot of our men do . . . they don't want to work overtime — it's not worth their while.

Indeed, the structure of the tax system in Britain encourages experiments in small business formation if only because of the distinction between schedule 'E' (which assesses the tax to be paid by employees) and schedule 'D' (used for the self-employed). Consequently, self-employed workers can claim allowances for expenses in a manner unavailable to those assessed on schedule 'E'. This point was rather amusingly illustrated by the owner-controller of a company with a turnover of £½ million and 70 employees,

> One of the reasons why these small businesses have started is that if they can get a smart accountant they can put their house down for tax purposes, they can put the dog down as a guard dog, they can get their telephone paid and they can get their car run can't they? It's from the sublime to the ridiculous isn't it?

Rather than restricting opportunities for the formation of business enterprises, then, the present tax system encourages workers to reject their employee position, to become self-employed and possibly, later, to become an employer of labour.

Once established, taxation is merely one of a range of factors affecting the expansion of businesses. But since taxation is an emotive issue for most small businessmen we will concentrate on the ways in which they *perceive* the operation of these taxes and how they *think* it determines the business decisions which they make. Thus, the way in which they *think* taxes work may, in fact, be quite unrelated to their actual operation and real effects. We are again confronted with a possible discrepancy between myth and reality. In fact, many business owners have a very poor understanding of the tax system. Even among those that do claim some knowledge, it does not seem to affect their personal motivation. According to Peter Rivard, a small employer, 'The way I look at it is if they don't tax one thing it will go on something else. If they give you any back you know jolly well it's come from somewhere else. It's got to balance. It makes no difference to me.' Similarly, for an executive director of a company with an annual turnover of £10 million,

> It [tax] certainly doesn't impinge upon our operations in any way at all. We regard tax as just a *consequential* thing upon our activities. Taxes arise which some day have to be sorted out. We often address ourselves to the problem of taxation and have to sort it out. It certainly does not influence our desire to do what we are doing. We think about it sometimes but generally we always overcome it.

Furthermore, many businessmen do not think that personal taxation has much effect on how hard they work. At most, if there is high personal taxation and a 'hostile' government – usually Labour – this creates resentment, reduces the level of job satisfaction and, hence, their personal working efficiency. The effects, then, are of a general psychological nature rather than of a specific economic kind. A small employer with ten workers was typical when he claimed, 'You can't work any harder. You give your best and that's your best. I don't think you can possibly work any harder.' Likewise, Cyril Lipton, a small employer with a yearly turnover of £50,000 told us,

> At the end of the year I have to pay tax. Okay, I might pay £5,000 this year and £10,000 next. You know, your tax goes up and down like a yo-yo every year, you have one good year so you pay more tax the next year, you have a bad year so you don't pay so much tax the following year. It goes back to do you put money to one side for paying your tax bill? No we don't. At the end of the year – God help us – the taxman comes along and says we only want a thousand pounds and you say 'Thank you very much'. But he might come along and say that he wants £5,000 and I think, 'Christ where am I going to find that from'. But taxes don't affect the way I run the business. Certainly, to take a few pence in the pound off personal tax doesn't make a scrap of difference, although it may affect the bloke with the weekly wage packet.

If, then, there is a widely-held opinion that taxation does not affect their *own* business behaviour, if only because it is considered to be a *consequence* rather than a *cause* of economic performance, different views are expressed about its effects on employees. As we have already seen, taxation on overtime is one of the major reasons for 'moonlighting' and for workers experimenting on their own. Many employers complain about this and it is often their major criticism of the tax system because it weakens managerial control. Harold Doyle, for example, a small employer with ten men, argued,

> We are never going to get out of the mire until taxes are cut. What's the good of working? Look, the chaps at eight hours a day, if they put in half an hour overtime, by the time I've taken the extra tax and social security contribution I'm just about putting my hand in my pocket to give them ten bob. They say, 'Let's forget it.' It pays them to earn less and go out at night time, a bit of moonlighting. The more the government meddles, the worse things get.

These observations had support from an owner-director with 60 employees who complained,

> A lot of the people who work for me, they come out with this business that it's not worth working on Saturday because they pay a lot more tax. If income tax did come down I would find it perhaps more easy to entice people to work overtime when they are required to. They would get a lot more money in their pay packets.

An owner-controller with 15 employees and £120,000 annual turnover, expressed a similar view, protesting,

> Taxes – they are all horrid! But the basic problem is that our chaps would all work on a Saturday if it was worth their while but by the time they've been taxed it isn't worth their while to work. And I think that's wrong. There's got to be something wrong there hasn't there?

Indeed. It seems that high taxation on income is more of an employer's than an employee's problem. While the one is unable to entice extra effort, the other can either enjoy more leisure or earn extra on the side. In other words, employers' complaints about taxation incorporate strongly-held grievances about externally-imposed limits upon their own managerial control. It is important to add, however, that the tax system is not only seen to affect the motivation of employees but also the enthusiasm of senior managers and the extent to which they are prepared to shoulder the extra responsibilities that often follow from business growth. As Stan Holdoway, the chief accountant of a company with an annual turnover of £20 million told us,

> It's very difficult to motivate people. There's lots wrong with our tax system. This latest 60 per cent top tax rate is fine for me but it's done very little for 90 per cent of our management. They're talking about cutting car benefits − it won't hurt me, I expect we'd vote another £600 salary to pay for the additional cost. But for my senior accountant or contracts manager earning £8,000 or £9,000 a year it's just one more nail in his coffin. He's crucified because everything is against the middle strata − the management stream. There's just very little incentive.

Employers are often concerned about the lack of incentive because it is seen as a constraint on business growth. This is also their major anxiety in considering the effects of corporate taxation. We therefore looked at the ways in which taxation can shape business structures.

We found there is often a tendency for expanding businesses to diversify and to set up relatively autonomous companies which operate as separate financial and fiscal units. One owner-director outlined the future of his company in the following terms,

> Looking at the accounts for last year we can see that we can be caught for so much tax. But rather than paying this, we could invest in all sorts of things. We are thinking of going into plant hire in order to lose some money that way. Also vehicle renting and leasing. We would have to form a separate company for that. We are also thinking of forming our own joinery and manufacturing company. This should all help our tax situation.

The owner-director of a highly diversified group of companies with a combined yearly turnover of £3 million, reaffirmed the effects of company taxation for the structure of his business when he claimed,

> It's all tax really. These smaller companies making smaller profits are taxed at the lower rate. So you see from a tax point of view it pays us to have these separate small companies which are taxed at a lower rate than if the profits were amalgamated into one holding company. That's the principle behind it.

Similarly, another owner-director added,

> From a tax point of view, if there's a massive loss in one subsidiary and a massive profit in another, then obviously before presentation of consolidated accounts we can shuffle around losses and profits to take advantage of the situation.

Diversification, then, is often a function of the tax system; it enables companies to disclose lower profits. But this policy is not always seen to be a tax advantage. As with most tax matters, it largely depends upon the specific circumstances of particular companies. The chairman of a group of companies with a combined total of 300 employees and a yearly turnover of £10 million claimed, 'It's really a management reason rather than a financial one in that it gives the directors of the associated companies a greater degree of flexibility and autonomy.' His chief accountant, John Bird, elaborated,

> There are no real tax advantages because really we are on a group basis for tax purposes so consequently, you can sift and shift them around and do what you like. In fact, you can have subsidiaries which are taxed individually or you can elect to go on to group relief which, quite honestly, saves you a lot of honest to goodness fiddling.

The complexity of the tax situation and the impossibility of making generalisations was emphasised by John Bird who felt unable to summarise the relative merits of various tax options: 'There are a lot of experts who claim there are disadvantages to group relief. I'm not too sure what they are. I know that sounds crazy but short of doing a very long analysis of the various Finance Acts I just can't tell you.'

The more important issue for a number of business owners is the way in which taxes create difficulties if they wish to realise their assets. They often feel the tax system does not recognise that they risked their own capital to establish successful companies and it gives them little opportunity to reap the benefits. They feel their control over assets which they, personally, own and have accumulated is now severely and unjustifiably curtailed. The owner-controller of a company with 30 employees and a yearly turnover of £1¼ million stated, 'Getting money out is always easier said than done. It's as difficult to get money out of this business, or any business, as it is to make a profit in the first place.' The owner-director of a business with £1¼ million annual turnover confirmed this,

Okay, the business becomes worth more on paper as it grows and expands but unless you can get some of the money out you might as well not have it. My analogy to this is the monkey who's got the nuts in his hand in a narrow-jar. It's very difficult to get any benefit from what you've generated in the way of capital growth. Immediately there are all sorts of things on it like capital gains tax. There again, if you invested that money you're going to pay investment surcharges.

The most comprehensive account was given by John Bird,

It's like getting blood out of a stone. It's almost an impossibility. You can get it out but you'll have to pay tax on it. If the owner takes it by way of salary then he's got tax to pay on it straight away. If he decides to sell some of his shares, he's got to find someone to buy them. But not many people are going to want to buy shares in a company where they have got no say in the damn thing. So there's no way he can get the money out that way. If the company buys him a lavish house, he can get caught for benefit in kind of some form or another. It's very difficut to get the money out because a company is also not allowed to make a loan to a director or share-holder. You can't say 'Let's give him an interest-free loan' because he's likely to come up against all manner of problems. There again, if you pay a dividend on shares there is this investment surcharge if your total dividend income is in excess of £2,000. You get an extra 15 per cent which is why the top rate of tax used to be 98 per cent. So there's not much point in dividends. So you can build the money up but you can't get it out. That is the problem. There might be the odd obtuse way which I don't know about. But basically to get the profit out of the company, there's no way you can legally do it. The loopholes have all been blocked over the past 20 years.

In other words, under the tax system, you are expected to accumulate but not to spend. If this point was brought out eloquently by a company accountant, the effects for the business owner were confirmed in the forceful words of Eddie Lawrence, a successful young owner-controller with an annual turnover of £½ million,

You just can't get the money in your hand — you can't blast it away. You can go and change equipment even if the old stuff isn't all that old. But you can't get tax relief on having parties and so on. If you could I've have them, don't worry.

One way of getting money out of the business is to 'go public', a path taken by George Arthur, an owner-director, in 1975,

> We went public for a number of reasons. One was the personal one; it was a good thing to become public so that part of the family who weren't involved in the company, but had shares, could get some benefit. By becoming public they could cash in without being so enormously taxed. That's the trouble with the private companies today in that it's more a game of monopoly than the public companies. At the end of the day, if you want any money in your pockets it's pretty unreal. By the time it's gone through all the taxation there's nothing there.

John Bird expressed a similar opinion,

> Normally, there are two reasons for going public: (a) the family can make some money out of it and (b) if your record is good enough and people buy the shares you put a hell of a lot of capital into the company. If the family sells the shares, then there's no argument about the valuation of the company for capital transfer tax. You've got quotations – no problem.

But from the owner's point of view there can be considerable 'administrative' inconveniences. To quote one owner-director,

> I personally very much enjoy the seclusion of a family business. I don't think I really want to share that with shareholders. I don't want to go through the formalities – the bureaucracy – of AGMs and all the rest of it. It may not be in the best social interests of the country but that's that.

But, as far as the future of companies is concerned, it is often felt that 'going public' will provide a more secure basis. As George Arthur explained,

> The advantages of being a public company is that it is set up so that the thing can run on indefinitely if there are good people there to run it. Whereas with a private company once the governor dies things seem to disintegrate pretty rapidly. There are a lot of good people

here and first-class management and therefore the very thought that the company can carry on if I'm not here is rather a nice thought. Whereas if we were a private company and if my son wasn't interested in continuing the operation I would be asking myself, 'What has it all been for?'

The effect of capital transfer tax on assets that are passed between members of the family is the source of considerable resentment. These were neatly summarised by one small employer: 'If I work hard all my life and I want to leave my son x number of pounds why shouldn't I? I mean aren't I allowed to look after the future of my own children?' Similarly, another small employer complained,

> As it is at the moment you can't give anybody a gift. I couldn't take money out of the firm and give it to my son – he'll have to pay tax on it. That should be done away with because you should be able to do what you like with your money in a free society.

Underlying these specific complaints concerning capital gains and capital transfer taxes, there is a more general resentment of any form of taxation which might be incurred upon death. This was precisely put by another employer, Dick Crook: 'You're taxed all your life on your income, on the products that you buy and then when you die, whatever you have managed to accrue, you pay tax on it again. I think it's terrible.'

From these opinions it is clear that the people we talked with have a very 'individualistic' set of beliefs. They regard taxes as a repressive imposition rather than a source of revenue for the welfare state. It tends to be only among the self-employed that taxes are regarded as necessary for essential social services. But, then, these people have not 'bought' themselves out of, for example, the state education and health systems in the same manner as the owners of the larger busi-nesses. However, despite their objections, we do not believe that taxes are a disincentive to entrepreneurship. Although they are always prepared to criticise the tax system in general terms, there is little evidence to suggest that this is affecting business owners' propensity to invest, take risks and generally expand their enterprises. We say this if only because of their almost complete lack of knowledge about the *specific* operation of the tax system. They are generally unaware of *exactly* how it affects their own business activities and consequently they are heavily dependent upon the specialist knowledge and advice of their accountants.

In the smaller enterprises no accountants are employed; instead, financial documents are submitted to outside firms. Only then do many owners have a clear idea of the tax to be paid. In fact, they conduct their businesses according to a range of personal economic and non-economic objectives such that the payments of taxes is often a *consequence* rather than a cause of these activities. It is also clear that for a number of smaller proprietors the non-economic goals are as important as the economic, and that 'outside' accountants are often more concerned about profits than the business owners themselves. In fact, it is almost as though the entrepreneurial role is delegated to the accountants. According to one self-employed person,

> The accountant expresses his opinion but it makes no difference. What he suggests is that basically I should charge higher prices — I'm just not making enough money. But I suppose I put a greater price on contentment than I do on financial gain.

Similarly, Peter Rivard, a small employer, told us,

> My books are away for audit now. The accountant will bring them back and say 'Look at your turnover — you're not making enough.' Money doesn't worry me. I get a satisfactory return but my accountant says it's not big enough. I don't get sufficient out but I'm happy, money doesn't worry me, I keep living and that's all I worry about.

Even the larger business owners seem to have a limited knowledge of the tax system. They cope with this by bringing in qualified accountants who are normally appointed as directors with responsibility for financial control. In some of the companies it is they who make the *real* decisions affecting future developments. The chief accountant of a large company, Stan Holdoway, described his function as follows,

> Because I'm an accountant I tend to play down the advantages of suggested projects. One has got to start from the other end of the spectrum and say it won't happen. Try and prove to me that it's a good idea. Somebody has got to put a financial regulator on these things. As a private company we have, after all, only got a limited capital.

In order to fulfil this task effectively several in-house accountants suggested it is necessary to explain financial matters to their owner-director employers in the most simple terms. As John Bird claimed, 'I've got practical men as fellow directors. You've got to put it in words of one syllable for them. It suits me down to the ground because they can then understand it — I am concerned that they understand something.' Eddie Lawrence, an owner-controller, confirmed the difficulties, stating,

I take advice from my accountant but the only thing is I can't work it out. I can work it out roughly in figures but it doesn't work out exactly the same. If it did, I wouldn't employ an accountant. It's because of my educational standard, you see. It's also my English — that's what I lack badly. If I had GCE English, I'd have it hanging on the wall, enlarged.

Many business owners, then, are not the financial wizards they are presented to be; they may take the ultimate financial responsibilities but they are often no more than the spokesmen of experts 'behind-the-scenes'. In a sense, this confirms a view of 'self-made' men who possess personal qualities of 'drive' and business 'nous' but who lack technical and detailed skills in financial or business matters.

Just as surprising as their limited knowledge of tax and financial affairs, is the degree to which many business owners are influenced by a large number of non-economic factors. In the previous chapter, we pointed out how often businesses are formed on the basis of a wide range of motives. Their later development can also be understood in these terms: profits are important but they are not the 'be-all and end-all'. Some of the owners are very wealthy and despite their complaints about capital gains and capital transfer taxes, they could sell their businesses and live comfortably. Yet they continue to work; to run enterprises that can create stress and demand considerable personal energy and time. Why, then, do they do it? As an owner-controller told us,

You say why don't I call it a day. Well I really feel that doing that is the easy way out. I think I'd become very bored. I feel that what I'm doing is still a challenge. I don't want the company to stop. I've put an awful lot into it and I'd like to feel that it was going from strength to strength, even when I'm finished and out of it.

Once companies have become successfully established, they are often regarded by their proprietors as economic entities in their own right. *The company*, then, has to be provided for, even after the death of the owner. This sentiment was reflected by the owner-director of a company with a yearly turnover of £2 million. He justified his role as follows: 'Obviously making money is a major goal of the company but there are other objectives as well. I see my own personal aim as keeping hold of and expanding the family assets with which I have been entrusted.' For others, to own a business provides sufficient personal satisfaction in itself; running in order to run. This seems to operate irrespective of the level of personal taxation. Thus, Brian Logan, the owner-director of a company with a £20 million annual turnover, told us,

Well, what keeps me going is the fact that I enjoy what I'm doing. I'd be bored to tears if I finished. I'd probably finish up physically going downhill – take to drink or run to fat. I enjoy the responsibility and I enjoy the challenge. Most of the new activities of the business really stem from me.

This attitude was echoed by his chief accountant Stan Holdoway who also reaffirmed the virtues of hard work for its own sake as a preferable alternative to domestic and leisure activities,

I get the enjoyment from having the adrenalin running. When I'm really in the thick of it, I just can't enjoy lazy holidays on beaches – I want to do things all the time. I get into trouble with my wife and family about it. I just don't like sitting around. I hate relaxation – if I do something, whatever it is, I've got to do it hard and never in a half-hearted way.

A number of businessmen emphasise the importance of producing 'good quality' products. As Keith Deane, an owner-controller with a turnover of £200,000, explained,

I don't need to be a millionaire. In fact I'm a little bit artistic and if someone gives me a challenge, then that's what I enjoy. Really, I'm a little bit over-zealous with it. I mean I tend to put the job satisfaction part in front of making money. It comes back to the fact that I only need enough. I don't particularly get satisfaction from just earning money although it's obviously important.

If there is a theme of social responsibility in Deane's comments, this is more clearly stated by Desmond Reid, the owner-controller of a company with 1,100 employees. He stressed that once established, a company should show concern for the welfare of its employees and the wider community. Again, profits and economic rewards, although important, are not everything. As Reid stated,

> We are an employer who endeavours to maintain the best elements of the family firm relationship . . . a personal relationship . . . where people count as people and are recognised and valued as such. We recognise that staff are our main asset . . . the primary area of responsibility, therefore, is to one's staff and operatives for whom a livelihood is being provided through the activities of the firm. To do this the firm has got to be conducted sufficiently efficiently to ensure that their livelihood will continue. Profit is, therefore, only a tool to enable a bit to be ploughed back into the necessary growth of the business and the replacement of its assets.

He continued this theme by stressing the contribution that a company should make towards the local community,

> For the community we owe it to deal with people in business in an honourable way and to the community, in a wider sense, of the town we live in. One tries to support local issues as they crop up. And beyond that, one needs to be recognised locally as providing an honourable service, a good quality result and something that is value for money.

The owner-director of a group of companies with an annual trade of £6 million made a similar point claiming,

> If you are running a company that is quite involved with the local community this keeps you pretty occupied. My father, particularly, has always been very much involved in the local community. I mean, he's an OBE and he got it not so much for what this firm has done but for what he's done in the community. Now I'm a magistrate and belong to the rotary club, yacht club, chamber of commerce and we act as trustees for various local charities. There are obviously business advantages if you are known locally but basically, for me, I do it because I enjoy it.

We began this chapter with the political discussions that assume businessmen are primarily motivated by economic self-interest and that the existing system of taxation restricts the emergence and development of business enterprises. Our discussions with business proprietors seriously question these assumptions. As we have shown, high taxation can actually encourage rather than restrict the creation of enterprises. Further, once established the effects of taxes on business growth are complex. Although they may determine the *form* of growth we found little to suggest that they affect *whether or not* growth takes place. What is noticeable is that the tax system expects owners to be committed to investment and growth rather than to consumption and the realisation of capital assets. It is, indeed, very difficult to take money out of the business without being heavily taxed.

The notion that 'self-made' men are *solely* motivated by economic returns is unfounded. As we have illustrated, many start their own businesses in order to drop out and to escape from the rat race. This is the motivation, with subsequent business success as an almost unintended consequence. Even for those running the largest of the companies we studied, the quest for profits is bounded by a wide range of personal, non-economic ambitions. If the tax system is *not* the determining factor as far as the growth of business enterprise is concerned, the much more crucial issue is the employment of labour. We explore this in the next chapter.

Notes

1. Bolton Report, p. 193.
2. Ibid., p. 349.
3. Ibid., pp. 195-6. Further, in their survey of the literature James and Nobes conclude that an increase in income tax, for example, 'does not necessarily provide a disincentive to work . . . it . . . could spur the working population to greater efforts'. Furthermore, 'it is quite possible . . . for the level of risk-taking to increase in the community as a whole when income tax increases'. S. James and C. Nobes, *The Economics of Taxation* (Oxford, 1978), pp. 70-1. For an insightful critique of the supposedly detrimental effects of inheritance and estate taxes on small business efficiency see, J. Boswell, *The Rise and Decline of Small Firms* (London, 1973), chaps. 5 and 11.
4. A clear statement on the Conservative Party's initial ideas on enterprise zones can be found in its publication, *Small Business*, no. 12 (September 1978).

5 THE MANAGERIAL PROBLEMS OF BUSINESS OWNERS

It is usually necessary to employ additional staff if a small business is to expand. An employer will only recruit employees if he thinks it will contribute to growing profitability. Nevertheless, some business owners are prepared to forego growth and the promise of extra profits precisely because it entails the employment of extra labour. In other words, attitudes towards the employment of workers will determine the extent to which the self-employed are prepared to relinquish their 'autonomy', small employers their direct involvement in the work process and within the larger enterprises, the types of organisational structure that owners will develop. But why do many business owners sacrifice the possibility of bigger profits through not hiring extra labour? Although the problem is sometimes financial in that it requires more capital, it is often mostly psychological. There seem to be two major anxieties which arise for many owners. First, the extent to which business growth limits their control over the activities of their enterprises. Secondly, how far they feel personally competent to cope with the organisation and supervision of labour.

Obviously, these worries are most strongly reflected in the attitudes of the self-employed but they are also found in the gut-feelings of many small employers. Alec Barton, one of the self-employed, told us,

> I just don't want to expand. I've had a taste when I had a couple of blokes and it's more trouble than it's worth. You can stay a lot better on your own. Even with one bloke working for you, it's a pain in the backside — you've got to find his wage. One day he's earning money for you, the next you've spent it — he's done something stupid and spent it all. I'm just not interested — I just want to earn a living and it's better to do that as self-employed.

For Barton, employing labour is an economic risk; it has to be paid for, and yet it can ruin the profits. By contrast, another self-employed man was reluctant to employ anybody because of certain *social* obligations which he felt existed in any employer-employee relationship,

> It's a big problem if you are employing a married man or someone

with responsibilities. If you are employing a youngster from school it's not so bad having to stand him off, but a man who only does one trade and has a wife, two kids and a mortgage, well you've got to think twice about standing him off. That's why I don't employ anyone.

Both these views may be an attempt to conceal an inability to handle employees. A number of the self-employed are primarily concerned to 'do a good job' for customers; they regard themselves as tradesmen rather than businessmen. They often recognise that they lack the ability to manage both men and finance. As one of them, Derek Bateman, stated,

I'm very much aware of my limitations and so I walk carefully. Mainly it's a lack of management ability. That's the whole of it. When my son takes over I'd rather have him organise it and let somebody else do the work. That's what I'd like to do – but I haven't been able to achieve it.

The administrative problems were reiterated by Cyril Lipton, once an employer with a labour force of more than seventy but now with fewer than six employees, who suggested,

The guys I've spoken to don't seem to think that they've got to keep books. This is where a lot come unstuck – they haven't got a clue. Just hard work doesn't make a successful business, you've got to have a good business mind. You've got to know how to negotiate, how to talk to people and how to do paper-work. So many fail because they just haven't got a clue of how to control or run a business.

Despite these worries, some of the self-employed do find themselves recruiting labour, often out of necessity (as they see it) rather than because of any desire for business growth. This often occurs if a tradesman has taken on too much work or because he doesn't want to keep his regular customers waiting. As one of the self-employed said,

I only employ another man when I'm so busy that I can't cope. Rather than let people down I'll employ him at not much profit at all. I might come out of it even or I might go down a bit. But on the other hand, the customer is happy and that's it.

Most of the self-employed we talked with have at least six months' work on their books which often *forces* them, despite severe reservations, to become employers. Even so, they are determined not to recruit too many workers because of the problems that might arise. As Barry Small, with four workers argued,

> With my 'happy band' I can do all that has to be done. I can do a manual day's work and cope. The moment I employ another man it means I've got to do more, I've got to do a bit more office work and I've got to start chasing round for more jobs. I would literally have to stop the manual part of my day and do purely supervision . . . I enjoy manual work, you see, and I enjoy it because I've got control of it. If I started delegating I'm going to lose contact, I'm going to lose interest. Something will suffer . . . It's really a very selfish way of looking at things. But then you've got to get something out of it . . . I've got to satisfy myself.

Similarly, another small employer with three workers claimed,

> I get interested in the job and I forget about the business side of things. I'm not ambitious to make a million pounds. I can tick along and I'm quite happy. If you take on more people so you start getting all the worries and the mental problems rather than the physical problems. You're running here, there and everywhere — you're guaranteeing a nervous breakdown.

This small employer is against expansion because of the extent to which he would be no longer able to exercise his own trade skills. The reluctance to become solely involved in 'administration' and 'paper-work' was reflected in the attitudes of another small employer with two workers,

> I couldn't delegate work more than I do — certainly not by having more employees. Because I like being involved myself. I like to do the jobs myself. You've either got to have two men and work yourself or have eight men and not work yourself. In other words, just supervise them.

These men are typical of the tradesmen who choose to stay small because they want to exercise their skills; employing more labour requires extra supervision which takes them further away from their trade. As a result, the problems of paper-work among the self-employed and small employers are often overcome by the use of unpaid family labour — normally their wives. As Cyril Lipton told us,

> I hate the paper-work but it is something that has to be done. I really only enjoy from 7.30 a.m. to 5.00 p.m. — the actual work. At the end of the day, you've got this pile of paper-work facing you. But, in fact, the wife does the majority of book-work for me. You know, the ledger, petty cash, invoices, wages, VAT and all that sort of thing.

There seems, then, to be a tension in the minds of many small businessmen. They must decide either to expand, employ more labour and throw themselves whole-heartedly into profit-making or remain as they are, with little or no labour and continue to work manually themselves. However, there are problems both ways. If they remain small with only a few employees, they often feel that they are over-dependent upon their labour-force. As a small employer stated,

> If you expand you've either got to do it in a big way or not bother so that you don't have to work as opposed to employing two or three and still having to work yourself. I think it's very chancy with anything below half a dozen employees — more chancy than going the whole hog and employing fifty people. I think the risks are far greater.

On the other hand, to expand also creates problems if only because of the difficulty of exercising satisfactory control over labour. As another small employer explained,

> You've got to take them and show them how the work has got to be done. We go and work as well on the job — it's the only way you can make things go. If we left it up to them all the time, it wouldn't. They'd go to sleep on it. You're not making what you should make on it. Whereas if we go, they work a bit harder.

The small employer knows that his relationship with his work-force has to change as the business grows but he is often very uneasy about it. There is a fear that employees will lose respect once he becomes solely an administrator and ceases to work directly with his men. Roger Sims, a small employer with an annual turnover of £100,000, described these tensions,

> There's only one way of managing direct employees in a small firm
> and that is to work with them. Never tell anybody to do anything
> that you cannot do yourself. You've got to be able to say 'Stand
> aside Jack and I'll bloody well show you.' That's the only way to get
> respect. My men know I can work as well as them but if they think
> they're carrying you they don't work half as hard. If they thought
> I was sitting at home on my backside five days a week they just
> wouldn't work.

Unless the small employer appears competent in front of his workers —
able to do any job — he feels he cannot justify his ownership of the
business. Without this self-respect he cannot control the output and
productivity of his workers and he has no way of cementing employee-
employer relationships. These anxieties discourage many employers
from expanding their firms. Each stage of growth tests their skills in
human relations and they often prefer to keep with their trade. Yet
many small businesses do cope with these problems. The owner makes
the complete transfer to administration and succeeds in developing a
new relationship with his labour-force. Thus, there is no need for formal systems of control as the employees can be 'trusted' to work efficiently. Repeatedly, the owner-controllers of firms stressed how dependent they are upon the 'trust' of their employees; in the sense of 'working hard', doing 'an honest day's work', 'a fair day's work for a fair
day's pay', and so on.[1] In short, the employees of small firms, in the
absence of managerial and supervisory control systems, are largely left
to 'get on with the job'. As Keith Deane, an owner-controller with 26
workers told us, 'People who work for me work on an element of trust
and as far as I can see, that's the way it's got to continue.' Similarly,
Ray Nichols, another owner-controller with 20 employees, said' Most
of our chaps have got to be able to work with a minimum of supervision — use their loaf. I mean they are fantastically good, they are very
responsible. You see, with us, we haven't got a big enough labour force
to employ supervisors.'
Supervision is undertaken personally by the owner-controller,
primarily through consultation and discussion with employees on the
technical matters of the task at hand. According to many owner-
controllers the employer should never *tell* the worker what to do; to do
so, would challenge the whole fabric that cements personal relationships within small firms. As Ray Nichols continued to suggest,

You must never belittle them. Treat them with respect – this is the biggest thing. Make them part of the team. Work with them. Discuss their problems and give them a pride in the job. If you've got to issue a bollocking never have an audience. If customers say your chaps are marvellous, make sure they know that they are appreciated. For example, if I went to a bloke and said, 'What the bloody hell are you doing?' he'd say 'Get stuffed, I've done my day's work and if you can't trust me, then fair enough!' You've got to trust them, providing they are capable. So the thing is to employ capable people and then treat them as adults.

If small firms, then, are heavily dependent upon 'trust' for keeping overheads low and for operating effectiveness, it is clear that anxieties about its breakdown can be a reason why owner-controllers may choose not to expand. These doubts were expressed by Alec Stephens who, with a manager and a general foreman, personally supervised more than 100 workers,

Everybody says you've got to delegate but once you leave your hand off the button then your business will start sliding. The main thing is to be on top of it all the time, in touch with every section and really on the ball. If you get to the size where you have to delegate, you've got to work *with* the person involved so that his mind works like yours and he's totally trustworthy. Personally, I don't want to get to that size. I don't want to get to the point where I don't know where the money's coming from and how different jobs are going. I don't want to get to the stage where I have to take somebody else's word for how the job is going.

The problems that arise with expansion were clearly expressed by another owner-controller with 30 employees,

I got to the stage where work wasn't being carried out satisfactorily. This came down mainly to supervision and the people I was employing as supervisors and general foremen. I've got to say, with regret, I didn't give enough thought when I picked out the people for these jobs. I delegated to the wrong people and made terrible mistakes. I didn't approach it in the correct way. I was not strong enough with people, not firm enough. It's so difficult when you start from the bottom and build up to the position I'm in now. You've always done things personally and when you see it being done by other people, you compare it to how you did it. I really don't like being an office man. I used to run around in the van and work outside and I still find it difficult not to become too involved.

Such were the supervisory difficulties that this particular owner-controller had recently been obliged to appoint a general manager, who told us,

> Up until last year the owner was really running the business on his own and was attempting to control the whole thing by himself. It just wasn't working – he was getting himself into a state. Maintaining control of labour by introducing 'in-between' management was the major problem. He tended to try and economise on supervisory staff, even on foremen and this aggravated the situation and didn't improve it. It was a question of getting over to him the need for capable control in the field . . . It was just a mushroom – a mushroom of chaos.

One way of overcoming these difficulties is to keep down the number of workers who are directly employed and to use self-employed sub-contractors. This is particularly common in the building industry and becoming more usual in other parts of the personal services sector. Instead of having managers, foremen and others performing the functions of supervision, 'the rate' for the job regulates output and productivity. Thus, the subcontracting system solves many problems for small employers; jobs are completed at pre-negotiated rates, while the impact of legislation in areas such as employment protection, labour relations and social insurance are drastically reduced. Consequently, supervisory control continues to be exercised by the founder-owner even though the scale of his operations may expand quite considerably. In plumbing, heating, electrical engineering, mechanical repair, garages, and in various sectors of the retail trade there is a general shift towards firms using self-employed, subcontracted labour. However, not all employers make widespread use of the subcontracting system. Some prefer to have a full-time labour force, even though this will entail greater administrative costs. The advantages were aptly summed up by an owner-controller with an annual turnover of £1¼ million,

> If we don't employ our own staff, there's no way we can stick to schedules. With subcontractors we would be at someone else's beck-and-call. We have control over our own employees and if we want

something done, we can manipulate our men in different ways towards that end. So control over what we are doing is the main
reason. It perhaps costs us more but we have the control over
where they go, what they do, when they do it and how they do it.

As the business gets larger, formal control becomes more of an issue.
The smaller employer's reliance on 'trust' is not sufficient and a new
administrative structure has to be developed consisting of managers,
specialist technical personnel and office workers. However, the owner-
director of these larger businesses are still just as anxious as the smaller
employers about delegation and 'trust'. For them, the central problem
of growth is the selection of competent personnel for senior managerial roles. Brian Logan, an owner-director claimed that it is almost
impossible to find people who are prepared to accept responsibilities
and to make fundamental decisions. As he stated,

> You have to have somebody who is keen and willing to take respon-
> sibility. There are still too many people who want to be paid for
> having responsibility but are not prepared to shoulder the conse-
> quences and to stand up and be counted when things go wrong. A
> lot of people go so far in a company and then they will just go no
> further because they are not prepared to take the responsibility,
> make decisions and get on with it. There's too much paper shuffling.
> Too many people are prepared only to make a decision and pass the
> ultimate responsibility up the line to somebody else. The essence of
> our business is having decisions made down the line.

On the face of it, Brian Logan seems to be prepared and eager to delegate areas of responsibility of senior management. On closer analysis,
however, it was clear his company was organised in such a manner that
it would be difficult for a senior manager to exercise much responsibility without first consulting the owner. As his company secretary
indicated, this is a particular characteristic of family-owned businesses,

> With a family company, selection to a certain extent, must be
> coloured by the people doing the selection. The decision inevitably
> falls upon the family. They have the ultimate say. In practice, the
> main board will probably make the decision but obviously, the
> owner has the major say — and quite rightly so. It's his money you
> are playing with. They'll decide whether you appoint or promote.
> The proprietor of a private company and his personality is all-

important. If you can't get on with them you may as well leave. You may as well go because, however good you are, you'll never make it.

The owner, then, has the final say because it is *his* money and *his* company that directors and senior managers are playing with. Consequently, he sees that he *has* to exercise close control, even if this is 'behind the scenes' of a decentralised organisational structure. As Stan Holdoway, the chief accountant of this particular company, put it,

> It's extremely difficult to communicate with the owner on a really open basis. This is true of most family companies – they keep their cards close to their chests and so it is difficult to know how they are thinking. This is the biggest problem in a family company, the chief executive and his word is absolute law.

The director of a subsidiary company of a large family-owned organisation put the problem another way,

> I believe that the owner feels he will put his trust in no one; that he must have a finger on the business and must watch everything that's going on. He must have all questions answered. Working in a family company, there are too many restrictions. You have to answer for too many things, for every decision you make – and by gum, you make an awful lot of decisions. This is a risk business and the only way to be successful is to make decisions based on instinct and experience. To go back to the owner with every decision leaves you floundering and personally, it can all be quite over-bearing.

Anxieties about delegation and 'trust' are not only reflected in the owners' control over their senior managers, but also in the development of company structures. While owner-directors are keen to give considerable autonomy to their senior staff and encourage their entrepreneurship, they are determined to retain control. One of the forms of organisational structure which allows both objectives to be fulfilled is the development of various subsidiary companies. Sometimes, this is a way of reducing tax liabilities but often it is a means whereby the directors of associate companies can exercise a degree of autonomy without the owner losing control. Although some businesses seem to be highly decentralised and fragmented, by being chairmen of holding companies and chairmen of each of the subsidaries the owners preserve their power and are able to exercise direct control over their groups' various activi-

ties. Since each of the subsidiaries will often be a separate financial
unit, it is fairly easy to pinpoint areas of profit and loss within groups
and to assess the performance of particular senior executives. Further,
competition — in terms of turnover and profitability — can be encouraged between the various operating units. As Howard Crompton, the
owner-director of a group of companies with a yearly turnover of £1½
million and 150 employees stated,

> We split the company up into subsidiaries for certain reasons. It
> enables you to see what A is doing and what B is doing although
> there's a lot of paper-work attached to it . . . It does enable us to
> see fairly clearly where money is being made and where money is
> being lost.

Often the senior executives of the various subsidiaries within a group
are not informed about each other's activities, except for the purposes
of creating competition between them. Identification with the subsidiary company rather than the group as a whole is generally encouraged.
As the director of a subsidiary told us,

> I've never been involved in financial meetings with the directors of
> the other subsidiaries. All I hear — and this is very bad — is when
> somebody is doing well or when things aren't so good. You may hear
> about it but you don't really know how bad things are. I've often
> commented about this, you see the holding company will use this to
> their own advantage but we would like to know what the figures
> actually are — whether somebody is doing well and then what do
> they mean by 'well'?

Similarly, the senior manager of an owner-director's company stated,

> In the relationship between the associated companies, there is a lack
> of co-operation between one and the other. It's perhaps because
> they think they are completely separate. The owner is really the
> only link between the lot. We've only had two meetings in the last
> five or six years where all the directors of the subsidiary companies
> are brought together. Basically, the only link between the companies
> *is* the owner who goes round everywhere.

In a sense, this is illustrative of a process of divide-and-rule which, at
the same time, reinforces the separation between ownership and con-

trol. Although senior directors are often offered a limited number of shares within their own subsidiary companies, this is rarely extended to participation in holding companies. The activities of holding companies, primarily concerned as they are with family investments and ownership, are generally kept quite separate from all other business activities. As an owner-director suggested,

> The group structure is really for management rather than for financial purposes. The management reason is that the holding company inevitably has all sorts of information about it that perhaps is not wanted and not needed 'down below'. Furthermore, 'down below' doesn't, quite frankly, know about it. So, it's a little barrier beyond which only the shareholders of the company penetrate. It's a rather secret sort of outfit – it's the family thing.

Decentralised organisational structures, then, may be relatively democratic enabling the senior directors of subsidiary companies to exercise a degree of autonomy, but they reinforce the personal control of the owner. Most owners feel there is a limit to the 'trust' that they can extend, even to the managing directors of their subsidiary companies. Furthermore, owner-directors often claim it is impossible completely to delegate the control function; they must know what is going on and hence, be competent in all areas of the business. This can determine the limits of business growth and the extent to which diversification will occur – even if profitable avenues of investment have been identified. The owner will only delegate 'so far', despite his employment of highly-qualified senior executives. This point was clearly stated by Brian Logan who emphasised the impossibility of completely separating ownership from control,

> At one point we diversified into areas where the management skills required were fundamentally different from those which existed in our normal business. We don't have the management ability to run a conglomerate. If we stick to what we know we can manage that effectively. I have come up from the bottom in this industry – I've been through all aspects of it – so people can't pull the wool over my eyes. So this is it – we've done our diversification and made a nonsense of it: in future, we'll stick to what we know.

This does not necessarily mean that such employers will impose rigid rules and procedures upon their managers. On the contrary, they often go to great lengths to create environments in which managers and executive directors are able to exercise initiative with a minimum degree of bureaucratic constraint. Control tends to be exercised on a personal, face-to-face basis within the context of flexible management structures. If textbooks on management behaviour emphasise the need for clearly-defined areas of responsibility and readily identifiable systems of supervision, we did not find this to be popular among the business owners we interviewed. On the contrary, they often deliberately choose to avoid such a system and to rely, instead, on personal and informal systems of consultation. As the senior manager of a large owner-director's company explained,

> The management plan we've got here is pretty rickety. It seems to work but there's no rigidly-defined management plan or structure. It sort of happens. Whether that's good or bad, I wouldn't know. If you read a textbook I'm sure it would say it was bad. But, believe me, it definitely seems to work here.

These opinions were also expressed by the financial controller of a company with a £10 million annual turnover,

> There's no great hierarchy of control which is rigidly adhered to. It just doesn't work like that, we don't bother with it. It's a very free-flowing sort of thing. We're all involved in other people's business to a certain extent. There's an interchange of ideas and conversation. We don't feel exclusive in our own particular function at all. If something major comes up, let's say a policy-type thing, the chairman steps in and we all have a chat and say, 'What do you think about this?' We make decisions on that sort of basis. But for practical day-to-day running, it's generally left to the director in charge, although we're all closely linked because we talk to each other frequently about problems and what should be done about them.

Rules and formal procedures, then, are seen to be largely unnecessary. This is understandable in view of the nature of the firms that we studied. The owners are 'self-made' men who have neither worked their way up management structures nor been systematically trained in management techniques. Further, all the firms — by modern standards — are small. Consequently, medium- and long-term plans as well as day-to-day decisions are the outcome of ideas evolved from the owners and by informal consultation with senior executives. To maintain this system there have to be 'shared' values and beliefs not only between the employer and his senior staff but within the company as a whole.

In the companies that we studied, including those with annual turnovers of around £20 million, we found there is a strong emphasis upon creating a 'family' or 'team' atmosphere. Indeed, most business owners emphasise that the creation and maintenance of such an environment is one of the most important aspects of their job. The excessive use of rules is seen as illegitimate and a heavy emphasis is placed upon 'trusting' employees to get on with the job. The 'loose' organisational structure suits both these purposes, providing 'flexible autonomy' for both senior and lower-grade staff while, at the same time, allowing the owner to intervene and to check performance quickly. It also helps resolve tensions that can arise over conflicts between 'trust' and close supervision. However, shared values are also very important; there is no place in small privately-owned companies for senior staff who do not agree with the owners. If disagreements are the basis for political intrigue within large publicly-owned corporations, in small private firms, dissatisfied employees often have only one option – to leave. It is this process of selection which frequently accounts for the alleged happy atmosphere of small businesses rather than the effect of size *per se* (as is often implied in many discussions). If the recruitment of staff is very important, so too is the maintenance of a family atmosphere. As George Arthur, owner-director of a large company, told us,

> My aim has always been to work as a team. I've always thought the team spirit is vital for getting first-rate people who will come along with you. My emphasis has been to ensure complete teamwork and our operation as one single family unit. If you worked here, you would be aware of it on your first day as soon as you walked through the door. You would find everybody fairly happy, pleasant and approachable. There are no barriers put up by anybody and if we have to have departments it's important to make sure the edges are blurred otherwise people build walls round themselves. It's important to take a stance whereby managers don't lock themselves up in an ivory tower. If it's necessary for them to make the tea, there's no reason why they shouldn't. I've always been at great pains to do the menial tasks, occasionally. I don't mind making the tea or watering the plants.

The effect of this policy was confirmed by the observations of his financial controller,

What matters is the atmosphere, the environment, the style of operation – and here it's still very much a family style. You don't get the
feeling that you're just a cog in a great big wheel. It's the sheer informality of the whole thing where one is involved in a very relaxed
and pleasant atmosphere with staff from top to bottom which is the
real attraction to me.

Such opinions were emphasised by a large number of the people we
interviewed who regard family firms as a solution to the problems of
modern industrial relations. These sentiments are reflected in a diversity of practices, all of which contribute to the integration of employees into enterprises and to the cultivation of shared values. To give
but two examples, an owner-controller with 60 employees told us,

I try to know all about my men, for example, if one's got a wife
who's ill or something like that, next time I see him I'll make a point
of asking him how the wife is. They appreciate it because it's the
only way they can identify and have an interest. We also, of course,
have a Christmas get-together and from time to time arrange an
outing.

In a similar manner, Keith Deane, an owner-controller with 26 employees, said,

Several of my men have had serious domestic problems which I've
been able to help them with. They remember it and it breeds very
good relationships. For example, one bloke found out that his wife
was having an affair with another bloke and he just wasn't up to his
job. So I asked him what was going on and over a period I was able
to get him straightened out. It was only a bit of moral support by
simply talking to him but he remembered it.

Among the businesses we studied, attempts to foster a family atmosphere sometimes lead to paternalism while in others, there are efforts
to integrate employees on the basis of an ethic of egalitarianism. Paternalism tends to be adopted in the larger firms while in the smaller
companies, egalitarianism is the more usual employer strategy. This
compares with the findings of other studies which have investigated
small workplaces. These suggest that with paternalism two processes
operate; on the one hand, the employer cultivates a close *identification* of employer and employee goals, while on the other, he stresses

important sources of *differentiation* between them. Farmers, for example, will encourage agricultural workers to associate their economic and social benefits with those of their own, while at the same time reaffirming the essential differences that exist between them.[2] The farmer *owns* the property while the worker doesn't and this legitimates the unequal relationship. Similarly, in the smaller enterprises we studied, owners encouraged employees to identify closely with their long-term interests although the unequal rewards would be legitimated not according to property, but by reference to the employer's *own* economic risks. As Eddie Lawrence told us,

> If you gave me a fiver and one of my blokes a fiver, I'd have fifty at the end of the week and he'd still have five. You can never share it out. But he's happy – he hasn't had to worry about his income and he appreciates me. He doesn't have any jealous streaks at all because he wouldn't take the gamble.

Equally an ethic of egalitarianism will be promoted by employers and stipulated on their terms. If employees are unhappy about this, so it was claimed, they can also take similar risks by starting their own businesses. Indeed, as we have shown in Chapter 3, worker resentment about economic rewards is often the reason why many start their own enterprises. Egalitarianism, then, operates within the context of 'satisfied' workers; others can leave – either to start their own enterprises or to work for somebody else. Nevertheless, this ethic of egalitarianism is circumscribed by the essential nature of the employment relationship. This was aptly put by an owner-director with 60 employees, who claimed,

> I try not to socialise too regularly with the people I employ. Of course, we have a social club, a darts evening, and we also have cricket matches which I play in. But I don't know everything about their families. I don't think that's a good principle to adopt. You see, if you've got to discipline somebody it's extremely difficult if you've been socialising with them the night before.

Indeed, the perceived dangers of excessive egalitarianism were vividly illustrated by Roger Sims, a small employer of ten men,

> I used to have two men working for me and I actually gave them vehicles. I said that they were for work but also for their pleasure,

so look after them. Within a very short time, they obviously thought, 'He's making a lot of money out of us, look at all his new vehicles.' And they became jealous and both left and started up on their own. So I've never helped anybody since.

Similarly, an owner-controller with a yearly turnover of £½ million told us, 'We help our employees in any way we can. But I'm afraid that it's like a customer relationship because otherwise you start to lose respect. As they say, familiarity breeds contempt, and it's right.' Despite the tensions in the egalitarian style, such an approach is almost inevitable given the small size of the enterprises and the personal experience of the employers who have generally been workers themselves and understand many of the sources of employee resentment.

From this discussion, it is clear that small businesses, as developed by their owners, are organised on the basis of informal and flexible personal relationships. There are a number of reasons for this, ranging from small size *per se*, to the nature of the commodity and type of technology used, to the personal experience of the owners themselves.[3] But the absence of any direct influence by trade unions is also important. By their nature, trade unions at the workplace have two consequences. First, they lead to the specification of work tasks, payment systems, and conditions of employment. Secondly, and following from this, they impose constraints upon what the employer can do with, as he sees it, *his* employees, *his* workplace and *his* assets. It is not, therefore, surprising that the owners of small enterprises are often hostile towards trade unions and that the level of unionisation in small businesses is low. But if small employers have, through various means, been able to avoid the 'dangers' of unionism, they have been less successful in withstanding the impact of labour legislation.[4] Legislation, for example, in such areas as unfair dismissal, redundancy and employment protection has, for the first time, constituted a direct constraint upon how the small employer can treat *his* workers. It is consequently seen as a challenge to the rights and prerogatives of employers and as a threat to the essentially egalitarian and personal style of small firms. The way in which legislation of this kind was alleged to have destroyed the informality of such enterprises was stressed again and again. For example, Desmond Reid argued,

In the past if somebody needed to be hauled over the coals, we would always have done it by talking to him straight out, man-to-man. Now, because of the employment legislation, you have got to formally have somebody in to witness what you've said and at the next stage give him something in writing to say that you've said it. Now this prejudices the closeness of relationships with staff. When you've got to do things legalistically it's quite out of tune with the way you wish to do it in the family firm.

Similarly, Paul Ewing, an owner-controller, stated,

Supposing something minor happens, in the past, you'd have had a bit of a row and that would have been the end of it. These days, he's got to have a record of it and so have you. Now that niggles him because it goes to his home and his wife finds it — I'm quoting actual cases now — she opens it and wants to know what it's all about. Then there's a row between husband and wife. Next morning he comes in and he's flaming mad. So it gets much worse than it would have been. Moreover, I think it's a very unmanly thing to do. I hate it because if you have a row with somebody you don't want it to be put in writing. If you're married and have a row with your wife you don't want it put in writing do you? That's about what you are having to do — it's like having a divorce.

Employment legislation not only represents a challenge to the informal nature of relationships within small businesses, it also affects the general attitudes of workers. This strengthens employee influence such that the owner is less able unilaterally to impose his own form of authority. The resentment which this creates was illustrated by an owner-controller, Alec Stephens,

Nowadays, the employee has the upper-hand. If you see somebody having a cup of tea outside break times you could, in the old days, tell him to pick up his cards at the end of the week. Now, you have to give warnings in front of witnesses and it makes things very difficult. So you think twice now about taking men on — you're frightened of taking more people. It's affected the general attitude of people. It's all different now — people used to be pleased to work and feel that they had to work to keep their job. Now, they come to work and this attitude just isn't there. They're not at all keen to impress. They know that if they lose their job they can make a claim and go back on the social security.

Consequently, it seems that the expansion of business enterprises is primarily determined by the extent to which the owner is prepared to delegate a number of his supervisory functions and how far he feels personally competent to cope with the organisation of an ever-increasing labour-force. With business growth there is a tendency for him to rely heavily upon 'trust' within the context of flexible and ill-defined management structures. Although this often gives senior management considerable working autonomy it enables the owner to retain control over *his* enterprise. He is thus resentful towards those influences which may, in various ways, challenge this autonomy. It is in these terms that his attitudes towards trade unions and employment legislation can be understood. Hence the pressure that small employers are exercising to amend legislation in these areas.[5] In this way, they hope to return to an employment situation in which informal and egalitarian work practices can be stipulated on *their* terms.

These, then, are the major tensions facing small businessmen when they decide whether or not to expand their enterprises. All this, however, presupposes the existence of markets within which they can trade. It is to the market situation of small businesses that we now turn.

Notes

1. We use 'trust' in a sociological sense. It should not be confused with the everyday connotation of personal 'liking' and 'disliking'. Instead, it refers to the 'trust' which resides in work roles and relationships such that the use of more rigidly and formally prescribed measures of work performance are unnecessary. For a scholarly analysis of the breakdown of 'trust' in present-day society see, A. Fox, *Beyond Contract* (London, 1974).

2. H. Newby, C. Bell, D. Rose and P. Saunders, *Property, Paternalism and Power* (London, 1978).

3. The personal services sector, as described in Chapter 2, has a number of characteristics that necessitate the development of 'trust' relationships if enterprises are to operate efficiently.

4. For a discussion of a small business owners' attitudes towards employment legislation see, R. Clifton and C. Tatton-Brown, *Impact of Employment Legislation on Small Firms*, Research Paper no. 6 (Department of Employment, 1979).

5. For example, the 1980 Employment Act exempts small businesses from many of the requirements stipulated under earlier legislation.

6 COPING WITH THE MARKET

One of the major factors that distinguishes small business owners from the salaried employees of large-scale bureaucratic organisations is their day-to-day involvement in the market. It is their ability to cope with the market that strongly influences whether they will ever be faced with the problems of expansion. Their success as businessmen is judged, not according to the number of their employees, but in terms of profit, turnover and market share. Although their attitude towards the employment of labour represents the major factor conditioning business growth this presupposes the existence of a market. This, in turn, is a major source of uncertainty and hazard but without it there could be no growth or risk. Market conditions not only affect the nature of a business, but also the owner's life-style, standard of living and society's estimation of him as a businessman. By comparison, although there is the ultimate fear of dismissal or redundancy, managers in large-scale corporations are often able to 'hedge' themselves against such personal uncertainties and to pursue rather more predictable career patterns. Indeed, personal fortunes and those of the employing enterprise can be quite separate, managers can pursue successful careers via a number of companies which may, according to various criteria, be in decline. For the business proprietor, personal career is inextricably tied to the success or failure of the enterprise. An owner-controller with a yearly turnover of £¼ million summed up the contrast between an employer and a salaried manager in the following manner,

> It was completely different when I was *working for* other companies. I was managing men but I wasn't managing money. Overheads didn't mean anything to me. I knew what they were but I didn't appreciate their importance. In your own business, as opposed to working for somebody else, it's your money out of your pocket every time. You're so vulnerable to the market. I suppose in a larger company you can get booted out in the end but there is a hell of a fluster before that happens.

Despite the hazards of the market few of the businessmen that we interviewed would have it differently. They subscribe to a popular image of the market which extols the virtues of free competition.

However, they still devote considerable effort to the pursuit of policies that limit their risks and exposure to market forces. The market, then, represents more of a personal philosophy accounting for the distribution of resources, the allocation of talent and skills, and the protection of the essential freedoms and rights of man in society. All of this was aptly summed up by a small employer with a yearly turnover of £80,000. He argued,

> It all comes back to individuals and human nature. Some people say we're all God's children born with the same opportunities and all equal. But that doesn't take into account human nature. At the other end of the spectrum is the Conservative principle based upon market supply and demand. Everybody finds their own niche in life and they work for what they are worth. If you work hard you get paid well or if you're clever, you get paid well. There's a free and open market where people *aren't* equal and that, really, is the only way to work.

Such attitudes are 'core' elements within Western culture; it is not surprising they are expressed by the majority of the people we interviewed. An owner-controller, for example, with a yearly turnover of £100,000, claimed,

> You will always get stability from supply and demand at the end of the day. Market forces will always dictate the situation, whether you like it or not. So you can't distort anything for any length of time. This business of the state ruling everything and controlling everything doesn't, in the end, work because it always distorts the picture. It's rather like having a set of traffic lights which don't work anymore and putting a policeman on point duty there – you always get more 'snarl-ups'.

However, a belief in the market does not necessarily mean that business owners will behave accordingly. All the proprietors we met had developed procedures whereby the impact of market forces might be reduced. The self-employed and the small employers attempt to create groups of regular customers to guarantee a steady flow of business and neutralise market fluctuations. This is a widespread practice within the personal services sector of the economy; shopkeepers, garage owners, publicans as well as independent solicitors and accountants develop their trade around 'regulars'. In many respects, such people cease to be businessmen in the accepted sense because they seem to give a higher priority to providing a service and ensuring customer satisfaction than to making profits and expanding the enterprise. Indeed, in this style of business the obligations and personal relationships between proprietor and customer can actually curb profits and jeopardise business growth; expansion entails more labour which, in turn, breaks down the personal nature of the relationship with the customer. Peter Rivard, a small employer with eight men, put these points clearly,

> I've got about 500 regular customers and I know them all. I've worked for some of my customers' grandparents and then their parents and now I'm working for their grandchildren. All my work is on recommendation – I don't advertise in anything. I don't have my name on anything except my bills so they know where to send the money. But still I've got six or seven months' work on my books and I'm refusing any more work – except for, of course, old customers. So I don't worry about competition. My price is my price – whatever anyone else throws in, I don't worry about. The major thing for me is to do the best job I can and to satisfy the customer. You see, most of my customers are friends and that's one of the reasons why I haven't retired.

For Rivard, then, business is part and parcel of a set of social relationships, he charges a 'fair price for a fair job'. 'Trust' binds the relationship and this in turn, conditions attitudes towards expansion as well as the kind of workers that he feels he can employ. He subscribes to a strong ethic of service, and of social contribution and this is as important to him as making money. He will not expand because this may reduce the quality of the personal service that he is able to provide. At the same time, he is careful to employ staff that are presentable and acceptable to customers as well as being technically competent; consequently the 'trust' relationship between customer and employer is not threatened. By doing a good job and providing a good service, Peter Rivard, and others like him, feel they can insulate themselves against the fluctuations of market forces. A small employer doing business worth £40,000 a year reaffirmed these sentiments when he argued,

> Basically, I only work in the immediate locality. Most of my work is personal recommendation and so it's not competitive. People come along and tell me they've heard I've done a job for someone they

know and ask me whether I'll do something for them. Then, whether it's accepted or not, just depends on whether they can afford it rather than my competitiveness. Price-wise, I'm not expensive but I wouldn't say I'm cheap — I do a reasonable job for a reasonable price. And that's what my customers want.

But there are problems when business and sentiment become inter-related, particularly within the context of rural areas and small market towns. Sometimes, the customer is seen to abuse the relationship because he wants something for nothing. This can be a negative side-effect of the friendship that binds the proprietor with the client. As this small employer added,

> Quite honestly I think the worst thing about running a business is working for friends. I mean it's terrible — if they ask you to do a job, they obviously want preferential treatment. They want a re-duced price. Then, when you get there, just to show how friendly they are, they feed your workmen tea about ten times a day and then you lose even more money. But my failing is that I'd sooner lose ten pounds on a job than lose a friend.

Furthermore, this same personal relationship can act as an obstacle to business growth if only because it disturbs the reciprocal nature of the 'trust' relationship. This was stressed by self-employed Stan Holmes,

> In a business like mine you rely on your customers and your cust-omers rely on you. If one rings me up tonight in an emergency it's my duty to give them a service. They've given me custom for 17 years and I feel I have to honour their demands. If we took on a bigger job it wouldn't be the same — we couldn't give this personal service. You find that businesses that get bigger and bigger just get more neglectful of the customer.

Similarly, another self-employed man with a yearly turnover of £30,000 claimed,

> The trouble is, we've got a lot of customers who are regulars and if we are on one job too long they may want us but we will lose them. You see, a lot of them are not just customers, they are friends. They know us — they chat away to Mum on the phone and yet she's never met them. But still they all know her as though she was a friend.

One of the problems of business growth, then, is the way in which it breaks down personal relationships. In other words, profit-making and capital accumulation would have to become the major goals with other considerations relegated to second place. Some business owners are prepared to make this move but the transition has many risks if only because old and well-established customers may not be easily replaced by new and more profitable clients obtained in more competitive circumstances. Further, expansion not only means a change in the number of customers but also differences in the type of customer; possibly a shift from private individuals to large-scale organisations. This not only affects the volume of trade but also attitudes towards the business. As Dick Crook, a small employer, stated,

> If I get extras coming up against a company, I consider that fair game. They expect me to charge for additional items whereas the public don't. They like a price and generally you try to keep to it. I've never charged extras against a private client. Against institutions — fine. These people expect to be caught, they expect that sort of treatment but the public don't.

A different morality then applies; companies and institutions are impersonal and anonymous whereas 'old ladies' and 'vicars' are protected by an unwritten, but important, code of ethics! A small employer reaffirmed the difference between working for private and commercial clients. He stated,

> If I'm working for a private customer I won't charge him what I charge a factory. I'd charge him, maybe, £3 an hour, but if I was working for a factory it would be nearer £60 a day so it's an entirely different sort of pricing.

The domination of commercial interests over all others, brought about by business expansion, was most clearly put to us by Stan Holdoway, the chief accountant of a large company,

> It's no good in this world believing you've got a personal relationship with a client — it just doesn't happen any longer. It's better that you both face up to the fact that I'm going to screw you for every penny I can get. For example, we were very good friends with a big local company. We always used to do all of their work and they used to supply most of our office equipment. But the fact is, other

people can do better deals on office equipment and they can often get other people to do work for them at a more competitive price. It's no use losing any sleep over it. The world is no longer the same. Sentiment has got to be put to one side – we are all in business to make money. He who allows sentiment to take over is going to catch a cold.

As firms grow, then, they become more rational and calculative in their orientation to the market. But only in the largest companies is there any attempt to develop a coherent marketing plan. By contrast, the smaller firms' dependence upon regular customers makes this unnecessary. For these, any expansion is often largely accidental or a response to somewhat unusual or unexpected business opportunities; even then, attitudes towards the further employment of labour tend to determine whether such opportunities are taken. With the larger enterprises, budgeting and forward financial planning are necessary if only to 'expand in order to stand still', given the high rate of inflation. However, it is the exceptional company that has a well-formulated marketing plan around which long-term strategy is organised. In one such case, Brian Logan, an owner-director told us,

> The main Board is the policy-making body of the group as a whole. Budgets are put to it by individual subsidiaries at the beginning of the year and once agreed, they're monitored by narrative reports and financial reports which come through monthly. As well as the twelve-month budget we have a two- and five-year general development plan and a rolling two-year budget. So it's a rigid budget for twelve months and then there's a rolling prediction of what's likely to happen.

More usually owner-controllers have little more than vaguely formulated ideas about business growth. Although they often recognise this to be a shortcoming, they rarely have any specific ideas of what to do about it. In fact, they often argue that inflation, high risks and the variability of market circumstances make nonsense of serious forward planning. However, some like Howard Crompton, the owner-director of a company with a yearly turnover of £1½ million, recognised the dangers of this philosophy,

> The thing that we've been slow on the uptake about is the necessity for marketing yourself. Just because here, in the area, we have a

good name, that's just not good enough. We've learnt that you've really got to advertise and market and provide what the public want — not what you think they ought to have.

With businesses controlled by the owners, it is not surprising that corporate plans are regarded as less significant than the ideas of the personalities in charge. Even among the largest companies the dynamic for expansion is often the personal energy and capacity of the owner. This, in effect, represents the essential characteristic of enterprises owned and controlled by proprietors; the fate of the organisation and the owner are closely interdependent. This has an important impact both for the system of delegation and decision-making (as discussed in the previous chapter) and also the long-term survival of the company; there is no attempt to cope with market uncertainties by formulating detailed forward plans. Some of these points were touched upon by owner-director, George Arthur,

From the time I was 30, job satisfaction has been the prime driving force — not the money side because I don't use that much anyway. Obviously, one has to make one's decisions according to what is good for the company as a whole but I generally find that the two go hand-in-hand. I get work satisfaction by becoming involved in new ventures and projects but this generally involves other people and they get similar satisfaction. So it's an important part of our policy that we become involved in interesting projects. We've probably done more pioneering than most other companies. We've an enormous record of, well, mainly failures because in pioneering you are more likely to lose money than make it.

A further reason why many business owners do not devote particular attention to forward planning is, so it was claimed, the general economic uncertainty created primarily by high inflation and government policies. Proprietors are reluctant to expand their enterprises in real terms and are prepared only to increase turnover and profits in line with the general level of inflation; to go beyond this engenders unnecessary business risks. The owner-director of a company with a £6 million annual turnover stated,

Our view of the situation at the moment is that we've just got to try and keep things going as they are at the present. We've a fair old struggle on really — just to keep the turnover, in real terms, steady.

We don't expect any expansion at all.

A small employer had a similar attitude,

> The last five years have been a difficult trading time — there's been a downturn in work-load. We've managed fairly successfully despite these adverse conditions. We've stabilised, consolidated and become established. If conditions had been more buoyant we would have made better progress — but as it is we're not looking for expansion.

But expansion for the larger companies is important if only because of its effects for the motivation and morale of executive and senior management staff. If, then, the owners of the smaller enterprises are geared to stability and market consolidation, beyond a certain business size, growth becomes an inherent logic of the enterprise. This point was strongly emphasised by Stan Holdoway,

> I believe that if you're going to continue to keep good executives there is only one choice in this world: to grow. Otherwise you go back to running the whole damn thing as a family company and the family will have to provide all the directorships and the experience and make all the decisions. We have got to go on growing otherwise you get rumblings down below and you lose people you would have preferred to keep.

The problems associated with inflation are inextricably linked, in the minds of many businessmen, with the general malaise of the economy and the failure of successive governments to cope with it. In this view the state has unambiguously failed to create the appropriate economic climate for business prosperity and growth and, indeed, has compounded this failure by 'meddling' with the free play of market forces. As we shall see, many of those who professed such views are not beyond 'meddling' with market forces themselves in order to protect their own interests. However, if the state engages in such activities this is unjustified 'interference' which creates additional uncertainties. Thus, there is a general feeling that, in the last resort, it is best for the market rather than the state to decide the overall level of economic activity. Desmond Reid, an owner-director, put the point as follows,

> People must be given the opportunity to use their initiative and ability to do what they think best. If that's taken away — if it be-

comes the responsibility of 'Big Brother' to decide what's best —
then growth is inhibited and needs are not recognised. Even if it's
bingo or dog racing — which may not be 'socially' desirable — if the
need exists in the *market* then somebody will jump in and meet it.
This is how you've got to live . . . Minimum government and maximum delegation of responsibility to the individual and the free
market.

Although such statements seem to suggest that the state should play a
passive role in the economy, many businessmen implied that they
would prefer the state to take an *active* part in creating a more stable
environment. 'Market forces are fine in general so long as they don't
affect us in particular.' Again, there is a discrepancy between publicly-
stated rhetoric and the personal assessment of concrete circumstances.
An owner-controller, for example, argued that,

The government has no regard for its responsibilities to this industry
at all. It picks us up and chucks us down again. There was a pro-
posal to monitor the work flow into the industry in order to cut out
the humps and troughs and to try and make it a more even work-
load. I would have welcomed that — it would have been the first
step to what we're after. We've got to find a way out of this dilemma
of the business going up and down — great surges of demand and
then suddenly nothing.

A stable market environment not only ensures greater predictability
in terms of risks and returns but also eases the intensity of competition
in particular sectors of the market. During periods of economic depres-
sion and falling demand, businesses often go 'downmarket' and take
work which would, in more prosperous periods, be left to smaller competitors. In larger enterprises this is regarded as 'ticking over'; covering
overheads and other fixed costs until market conditions improve when
more expensive or complicated work can again be undertaken. However, it can mean death for the smaller company. Desmond Reid, for
example, recognised this danger although he suggested that his own business was sufficiently protected,

At our size and level of turnover we are 'pig in the middle' really
which is a dangerous situation. The way we're placed at the moment
the market available to us is not being pinched *too* heavily. It is to
some extent, because orders tend to be smaller than they were a few

years ago. The very big orders are fewer and so the bigger businesses are looking into our market more. But it's the firms slightly smaller than us, with less reserves, who are in the real danger.

However, Dick Crook, a small employer, had felt the full force of 'unfair' competition from larger businesses,

There are two or three local firms which I class as the next stage up from my sort of size. They tend to be more expensive than me but at times when they're short of work their prices come down drastically. They can afford to do it just to keep the labour – to keep the men ticking over. So prices have gone down, material costs have gone up and the profit margin has been really squeezed.

Before our interviews were concluded Crook had, in fact, closed down his business and left the area entirely. No doubt others we met will have similar experiences because, for those working on their own or with only one or two employees, the intensification of competition derives not only from larger businesses but also from the tendency for potential customers to 'do it themselves' rather than pay to have a service provided. Although 'do-it-yourself' is associated with household maintenance, repair and improvement, it in fact covers a much wider range of activities. When individuals see to their own financial accounts, convey their own homes, service their own cars, entertain at home, make their own beer and knit their own sweaters, then accountants, solicitors, car mechanics, restauranteurs, hoteliers, publicans and shopkeepers have all, effectively, lost business. This takes us back, once again, to the 'informal' or 'hidden' economy which may threaten the survival of those struggling at the lower end of the formal market whilst *at the same time* acting as a seedbed for the formation of new small businesses. Competition of this sort is frequently perceived as unfair by those running larger companies because of the additional costs and overheads which they have to bear as a result of their 'legitimate' status in the market.

If the state cannot be relied upon to soften the impact of market fluctuations then there are various strategies which might enable individual businesses to reduce the uncertainties and risks. For larger businesses, diversification represents one possible means of spreading risks and ensuring a greater continuity of demand. The financial controller of a business with a £10 million turnover, explained recent developments within his own company in the following words,

Looking back at the history for a moment, 99.9 per cent of our profits came from one line of business. It really took off in the post-war period and there was no need for diversification, there was sufficient opportunity for expansion in this particular game. Now the whole position is changing very rapidly. There are strains in this sector of the economy and a very low level of production so we need to diversify. It's not sensible to have all your eggs in one basket because it can go wrong.

But there are constraints upon diversification, even when there is money available to invest (one of the companies had £1 million in cash reserves but had been unable to find a satisfactory business opportunity). In the previous chapter, we discussed the way in which owners will not develop activities in those areas in which they do not feel personally competent; despite the fact that they may have highly-qualified managerial staff and have taken advice from marketing experts. As the company secretary of a business with an annual turnover of £6 million told us,

In 1976 we brought in some marketing consultants to see how we were placed and what prospects were for our business. They advised us to diversify into the electrical business and also into engineering. The engineering was a bit of a disaster because our management skills weren't compatible with those needed in that line of business.

But other considerations are also important and, in particular, the problems associated with the employment of labour. Most of the business owners will only consider diversification into areas where the employment of labour can be kept to a minimum, even in the face of potentially high financial returns. Howard Crompton stated, for example,

Unless you've got a set-up where you know your people – you know who you are going to employ – the market can be literally more trouble than it's worth. Our tendency has been to think of a marketable product which doesn't get us involved in too much of a labour problem.

In a similar vein, another owner-director argued,

I'm looking for an investment right now but one thing it will not be is an investment that employs labour – that's a headache. I would be reluctant to take on a diversification that involved a big degree of labour and management, particularly in a strange industry. If you are going to diversify you must know something about it or else get a straightforward, non-involvement type of investment. For example, our highland land in the North of England – I mean, honestly, you don't really have to manage grass do you? You just don't worry about it.

One popular alternative strategy is to acquire reliable staff and an entry into a new market by buying out smaller companies. Brian Logan, an owner-director, had bought a number of companies because, 'Primarily in our business you're buying a tested labour-force which has been proven over the years and also, in many cases, a very competent management.' When there is a perceived shortage of managerial and skilled labour, this is obviously a rational strategy, a managerial team is acquired and the difficulties of creating decision-making processes and patterns of worker supervision and control are reduced; in other words, the business is 'already there'. But the acquisition of companies is also a good marketing strategy if only because 'goodwill' relationships with customers, and 'contracts' within specific industries are already well established. The marketing advantages of diversification through acquisition were emphasised by Stan Holdoway,

> In my opinion, it's better to take over small family companies already established rather than going 'cold' into an area and trying to build it up from scratch – particularly if you are in a situation where there's no growth. For example, we bought up a business in Norfolk primarily for the goodwill and the contacts that you need to make sure there's a flow of work. Within days we had a flood of work coming through the door which we would never have otherwise got. So, its a marketing thing – we're established.

Likewise, the marketing manager of a company with a yearly turnover of £12 million, stated,

> It's very difficult going into an area cold. It's far better, if you are going to expand, to buy into a company that has business connections. If that company has good connections and a good trading situation – and assuming there is some goodwill – then this, definitely, is the right thing to do.

Such an approach to expansion reaffirms the utility of the management structures that we discussed in the previous chapter because it favours the development of de-centralised associated companies operating under the direct control of the owner. But such structures are also determined by conditions of the market; it is necessary to adopt management systems that are adaptive and flexible. In management textbooks, two organisational models are presented – the 'mechanistic' and the 'organic'.[1] The former is characterised by a fairly rigid stipulation of procedures for the purpose of delegation, supervision and decision-making. Work tasks are clearly defined and allocated within the context of a readily-visible hierarchy of authority. The 'organic', by contrast, is much more flexible; job descriptions are deliberately kept vague and there is no firmly-established division of labour. Instead, directors, managers and supervisors are expected to be highly adaptive in terms of decision-making, carrying out work tasks and generally coping with business fluctuations and uncertainties. For operating efficiency, there is a tendency for companies in fairly stable markets to have rigid 'mechanistic' forms of management while those in circumstances characterised by high risks and uncertainties assume the 'organic' model. In our own study, 'organic' management structures were apparent in all the larger companies. This, no doubt, is reinforced by the dominant role of the owner-directors and their reluctance to delegate, and 'bureaucratise' managerial procedures. The owner-controller of a company with a £½ million annual turnover, illustrated the link between market conditions and management structure when he stated,

> There's no continuity of work in our business. There's no stability of work so we can't keep a stable labour force or a stable system of management procedures. That's the problem in this business, you've got to have managers that can muck in and adapt to changing circumstances.

Diversification, then, is a strategy well suited to the growth needs of the larger companies. Among smaller businesses alternative approaches are to cultivate 'gentlemen's trading agreements' with personally known competitors, or long-term trading relationships with large commercial organisations or public authorities. This is a widespread practice, not only in the personal service sector but also in manufacturing industry. A large proportion of small engineering firms, for example, produce specialist components for large assembly companies. Legally, they operate as autonomous enterprises but in *real* terms they are often little more than 'satellites' dependent upon one or a few large companies.[2] Similarly, among the smaller companies we studied we often found a dependent relationship with larger customers. This has both advantages and disadvantages. On the one hand, it provides a guaranteed volume of business which aids the rational planning of manpower, raw materials and work tasks. It also enables more predictable calculations about profit margins to be made. But although, by these means, an enterprise can 'opt out' of the market, difficulties arise if it becomes too dependent upon one or two large customers. As a small employer explained,

> Since 1972 we were maintaining and servicing a local factory which has just closed down. That was worth £30,000 a year to us – and our total yearly turnover was £40,000. That's gone, just like that. So it's a bit difficult at the moment because we are virtually starting all over again. As a result, we've had to start advertising in the last few months.

The closure had thrown this business back into the market; the proprietor had to advertise and tender for jobs. These were activities in which he lacked expertise and consequently he had considerable doubts about the long-term survival of his business.

There are, then, a number of procedures whereby small businessmen attempt to isolate themselves from the full rigour of market forces. As we have attempted to show, these vary according to size of the enterprise. The self-employed and the smaller employers often cultivate a large number of personally known, regular customers with whom 'fair' business is conducted. Among the larger enterprises, more calculative measures have to be used, including diversification into associated areas of business activity and the acquisition of smaller firms.

These various strategies are symptomatic of an interesting paradox. While at the general level all the business owners believe in the market as the basis for an economic system, a significant proportion of their time is devoted to avoiding its effects. Nevertheless, a *belief* in the market is crucial for a number of reasons. It can, for example, 'legitimate' falling profits and a decline in trading activity since these can be attributed to 'adverse' market conditions rather than to incompetent decision-making. It can also be an important mechanism for defusing employer-employee tensions about 'acceptable' wage levels. A number of the companies we studied were confronted with acute shortages of both skilled and unskilled labour which, in some cases, affected the potential for growth. Anyone believing in the virtues of market forces would be inclined to suggest that the problem could be resolved by increasing the 'rate' for the job. Often, this policy was not adopted, however, on the grounds that it would lead to a loss of competitive advantage, particularly for smaller businesses. This point was clearly illustrated by Keith Deane, an owner-controller,

> I honestly believe that the men in our industry just aren't paid enough. But I can't do anything about it. Why not? Because I'm in competition and I think if I paid them a bit more money we wouldn't be getting the business we do.

The market, then, is functional for 'harmonious' employer-employee relationships because it can be used by the owner to account for the level of wages. In other words, he can argue that the market does not allow him to pay more, yet he can still be seen as a 'fair employer' in the eyes of his employees.[3] Further, as we have seen in an earlier chapter, he can 'legitimate' his own higher economic rewards by reference to the risks he is prepared to take in the market.

So far, we have discussed market factors solely in terms of the sale of commodities. We have ignored the market for credit. The reason for this omission is quite simple: it is of little importance for most of the business owners in our study. The Wilson Committee's Report on the financing of small firms comes to the same conclusion in discussing the service sector,

> The evidence from this survey is that finance is far less of a problem for small service firms than the overall economic environment in which they have to operate. There were few significant complaints about the financial institutions with which small firms deal — mainly the clearing banks . . . The principal sources of finance both for starting a small service firm and expanding it are the resources of the founders, and to a lesser extent their families, and the clearing banks. Other financial institutions . . . are relatively unimportant . . . lack of external finance was not regarded by respondents as a major constraint on the expansion of small firms . . . The overwhelming majority of the sample were very satisfied with their relations with their bank, although some improvements were suggested.[4]

Most of the businesses that we studied started with negligible assets and their subsequent growth was largely self-financed, supported by bank overdrafts. These bank facilities are often a crucial back-up in the early stages but business growth is generally financed through the reinvestment of profits. The attitudes of Desmond Reid were illustrative of this,

> We've ploughed all our profits back into the company. The business has grown entirely from within. There's been no other source apart from the odd project where specific financial arrangements have been made and then dissolved. And so there's no continuing outside source of finance. This is desirable as long as the private company can find access to such funds it needs in order to do the things that are part of its natural pattern of operation and growth. It means you have complete independence and freedom of action. You are controlling your own destiny . . . We want to go on doing the thing our way . . . That's why we don't go public.

This enthusiasm for self-financing keeps ownership in the family but it means the owners are often required to sacrifice or defer a higher level of personal consumption in order to expand their companies. An owner-director with a yearly turnover of £3 million told us, 'We've always put everything back into the business. It's the only way. I mean, if you take it out, you won't have it in order to expand.'

But it is also necessary to have cash reserves on hand in order to meet market fluctuations. As Peter Rivard, a small employer argued,

> I've never ever been dependent upon credit. I've never had a loan of any sort — never had anything at all in that way. I've just kept floating and building the business up slowly. The money goes back all the time in the business. I don't keep any other accounts than those in the business. Because you can be on top of the world one minute and think you're well away and then work can go wrong, and you are down low on reserves again. So you've got to keep something in hand.

At most, the men we interviewed had only negotiated short-term credit facilities with banks in order to tide them over exceptionally heavy investments and for financial protection should customers fail to pay promptly. An owner-controller with an annual turnover of £¾ million stated,

> Our overdraft facility is £50,000. We used that once when we were

doing some work which took some time to sell. In general, I'm on very good terms with the bank. My bank manager and I are good friends – he even comes here and plays snooker with me.

Similarly, owner-controller Alec Stephens claimed,

We could run our overdraft facility to £120,000 but we are nowhere near that most of the time. If we ever do need to go up to, or even over, the limit we have to telephone the bank and warn them. Providing we warn them and give them reasonable reasons, they've always been alright.

On the whole, then, access to credit is no problem. Indeed the findings of the Wilson Committee on businesses in the personal service sector were re-iterated by Howard Crompton,

I think the greatest difficulty of further expansion is not finance, although of course you've got to be careful. Any fool can borrow money, there's no trouble about that. Our biggest problem of expansion is to get the right sort of regular labour force, and for a business our size, it's a jolly worrying problem.

This, then, concludes our discussion of business owners in terms of the ways in which they own, control and finance their businesses. So far we have considered them at the workplace and in the market, but they also participate in family and community relationships and furthermore, have strongly-held views about the way in which society is, and should be, organised. We turn our attention to these matters in the next three chapters.

Notes

1. T. Burns and G. Stalker, *The Management of Innovation* (London, 1961).

2. A Friedman, *Industry and Labour* (London, 1977).

3. Newby and his associates, in a similar manner, show that farmers often argue to their employees that they cannot afford to pay more wages because consumers are unprepared to pay higher prices for foodstuffs. See, H. Newby, C. Bell, D. Rose and P. Saunders, *Property, Paternalism and Power* (London, 1978).

4. Committee to Review the Functioning of Financial Institutions, *The Financing of Small Firms*, Cmnd. 7503 (London, 1979), pp. 54-5.

7 FAMILY, CONSUMPTION AND STYLES OF LIFE

The entrepreneurial family functions quite differently from the normal Western pattern. Generally speaking, the 'typical' family spends money but does not earn it. Wages and salaries are earned through employment in the occupational structure and then largely spent, within the family, on day-to-day subsistence, leisure and recreation. Although the family is outside the formal occupational structure it nevertheless performs important 'servicing' functions. For example, it is within the family that a wide range of unpaid personal services are undertaken which enable individuals to perform their jobs and ensure their eventual replacement by future generations. Further, the family is generally regarded as the essential outlet for emotional and personal relationships; as a retreat from the rational, impersonal and instrumental behaviour expected within the occupational structure. In a variety of ways, therefore, the modern family in its *private* life complements the *public* economy and helps it to function effectively.[1]

This sort of analysis does not apply to the entrepreneurial family where the fusion of production and consumption has important consequences for family relationships, expenditure patterns and the use of domestic assets. For most workers, income is determined by the wages or salaries paid by employers and all major domestic decisions focus upon expenditure – on such items as houses, cars, consumer durables and holidays. But for the entrepreneurial family, expenditure parameters cannot be regarded as given; on the contrary, there is a constant need to decide how much income can be privately consumed and how much re-invested in the business. There is a direct trade-off, therefore, between living standards and business development and, to some extent, one has to be sacrificed at the expense of the other.

A further important difference derives from the manner in which family labour and property are used to support the business. Indeed, in the personal services sector many enterprises like shops, restaurants and hotels are only profitable because the overheads are subsidised by the unpaid services of family members and by the use of domestic facilities to accommodate the business. In this situation it is difficult to make any clear distinction between domestic and business life. In fact, the fate of one is highly dependent upon the fortunes of the other. While divorce can destroy a business, a successful relationship between husband and wife can be a vital base for business growth. Indeed, we would argue that the nature of marital relationships is crucial to any understanding of the formation and growth of small businesses. Furthermore, wives can determine to a large degree whether an individual will become self-employed and how far private savings, domestic amenities and family labour will be available to the business. Thus, fundamental decisions concerning the allocation of resources and the domestic division of labour are often the outcome of husband-wife negotiations.

In establishing an enterprise it is often the case that part of the home is surrendered to the business. Many of the people we interviewed had started their business at home using a bedroom as an office and the garage as the stores or workshop. This immediately impinges upon family life and domestic behaviour, which are constrained in order to underwrite the initial costs of the business. The priority given to 'business' over 'pleasure' was reflected in the recollections of one of the self-employed,

I had a van which I bought prior to starting on my own. I bought a van rather than a car because it was, in my mind, always a necessary tool. From the money point of view I started with two weeks' wages and also used a week's holiday money.

Occasionally, even quite a large business never leaves the home. An owner-controller with 60 employees, for example, continues to run his £¾ million business from a desk in his living room. Even after substantial business growth, it is often difficult for the small businessman, his wife and particularly his tax inspector, to separate domestic and business assets.

If domestic amenities are frequently sacrificed for the good of the business then so, too, is time. In the initial stages of a business, when little or no labour is employed, the working day often extends from eight in the morning till six in the evening, with two or three additional hours after the evening meal. Typically, physical or manual work is undertaken during the day and paper-work is completed in the evenings or at weekends. Peter Rivard, a small employer with eight workers, described his normal routine as follows,

My working day starts at seven-thirty in the morning until six. I come home and some evenings I might work from about nine till ten-thirty 'booking-up' and also, nearly all day Sunday 'booking-

up' – from about eleven in the morning round till perhaps ten at
night, except for the odd walks with the dogs in between. I used to
work more than this – most evenings it was from seven till ten-
thirty – but I don't do quite so much now that I'm getting older.

For Peter Rivard, then, there is little time for pleasure, in fact, his
business *is* his pleasure. This is a similar pattern to that of another
small employer,

> I leave home at seven-thirty in the morning and we start at about
> eight. Lunch break is only about thirty minutes. I tend to take a
> packed lunch, because I can't stand sitting around. Then I work on
> till five and then I get things ready for the morning and so by the
> time I get home it's half-past six. In the evening I find myself having
> a meal and then doing a couple of hours' paper-work every night.
> Then, of course, there's Saturday mornings – that's mainly manual
> work but sometimes I have to take the whole day to really get on
> top of the paper-work.

What is clear from these statements is that most of the self-employed
and small employers undertake a normal, *productive* working week
which is supplemented by evening and weekend work when all the *non-
productive* administrative activites are undertaken. This sort of life puts
a tremendous strain on family relationships but it is often an essential
'investment' in the business. Without such unpaid extra work many
businesses would collapse – a point which was emphasised by Cyril
Lipton when explaining how he costed his own time,

> It's a long week, but basically I only cost from seven-thirty till five.
> You can't bring in what you do at night-time and weekends. If you
> do, you might as well pack up because at the end of the day, your
> work would be costing so much that you'd be uncompetitive.

Like all investments the small businessman's unpaid labour has an
opportunity cost – in this case, family relationships. Eventually there is
always the hope that things will improve as the business grows. In the
meantime the whole family, and especially the wife, may have to accept
a difficult time and, in effect, subsidise the business. All these problems
were aptly summed up by self-employed Mel Morgan,

> This job involves some bloody hours – probably 85 hours a week.

You never know when to stop working. It's never away from your mind. The phone never stops ringing and the aggravation you get from stupid, irate, bloody customers. I've got so much work and not enough time. We want to take the kids to Disneyland. We want to do lots of things. We want to *start living*. I want to see my children – they're growing up around my ears and I don't even know it. Sometimes when I leave in the morning they're still asleep and when I get home they're in bed. I don't *see* them – it's no way to have a family. In fact, it's been no life for the last ten years. We've been nowhere. We're going away for a week this year – if we hadn't booked that, we wouldn't be going.

However, as the business expands and the owner withdraws from physical or manual work to concentrate on administration, a clearer distinction between 'family' and 'business', 'work' and 'leisure' and 'home' and 'office' emerges. Business premises, separate from the home, are acquired and there is a decline in the extent of unpaid labour undertaken by the owner and his wife and family. But typically, dedication to the business continues and owner-controllers and owner-directors often *choose* to work long hours and take on heavy commitments when, in effect, they have the option of an easier life. According to these men, there is no possibility of a middle way: owner-directors in particular have to be either involved or completely withdrawn from the business if confusion and inefficiency are to be avoided. 'Total involvement' is the course which many owner-directors choose for reasons which were clearly summed up by Stan Holdoway, the chief accountant of one of the larger companies,

If you are a family company and the chief executive spends most of his time on the golf course or sailing or whatever, you really do lose some of the spirit. But if you can get the chief executive on the phone at eight-thirty in the morning and if the light's still on in his office at seven at night, it sets the tone. If the chief executive wants to get out it must be total and clear, you can't have this half-hearted thing where, in theory, he's the chief executive but he's never there and he leaves the poor old deputy managing director to do all the donkey work. It does happen in some companies and that's usually when they start to fall apart.

As the role of the business owner changes with the growth of the enterprise so too does that of the wife. Amongst the self-employed and small employers, wives not only make substantial domestic sacrifices, they also provide a crucial source of unpaid labour. Usually the wife is responsible for the secretarial work and the book-keeping which has to be fitted in with other household duties. In effect, she often has *two* unpaid jobs — housewife and administrator — and her contribution can be crucial to the success of the business, as one of the small employers pointed out,

> My wife does all the wages on a Thursday night and the end of month accounts. She looks at the mail in the morning and shoves the invoices in the envelopes. She also answers the 'phone and keeps people away from me, if you know what I mean. If I didn't have her, I would have to employ somebody which would cost me, at least, £3,500. This is one of the perks of the business in that I can show my wife as earning so much money on the books, but, in fact, she doesn't draw any — it's still kept in the business.

Similarly, another small employer claimed,

> I would not be able to carry on the business without my wife. She deals with *all* the financial side of it. I would have to employ somebody to do what my wife does. But then, obviously, it's in both our interests so we're both pulling for the same thing. I don't know whether you would get the same commitment from an employee.

As this statement suggests, the wife is often much more than the office manager, she becomes, in fact, the real financial decision-maker. Many of the married women we met had some relevant experience as ledger clerks, book-keepers and, sometimes, as assistants in firms of accountants. As one small employer explained, this can be very useful,

> I do detest paper-work, although my wife does all the books side of it. I may scribble out an account but she will take over from there. She was an accounts manageress — although I didn't marry her for that! I think a lot of our success is due to her. She earns most of the money. For example, she'll 'phone around to get the right quotations for materials. If you don't buy at the right price, you can't be competitive and sell it and make a profit.

Women, then, are indispensable for the small business; they are the hidden investment which is almost totally ignored in biographical and autobiographical accounts of highly successful 'self-made' men. From our discussions it is clear that their role in the business makes it almost impossible for them to pursue independent careers. Hardly any of the married women we met have either part-time of full-time jobs outside the business. Furthermore, husband-wife relationships within the family are 'traditional' and characterised by a rigid division of labour. Because of the time devoted to the business by the husband, the wife undertakes almost all of the domestic tasks and is largely unaided in looking after the children and spending the household budget. In many ways, there are similarities with the one-parent family. Occasionally a wife without dependent children is able to pursue her own career but this is usually *within* the family business – as part and parcel of a process of small-scale diversification. One example of this was Mrs Sims whose husband, a small employer, told us,

> My wife's shop is far more successful than our original business because of the effort she's put into it. It was a new venture for her – and having been company secretary and having dealt with customers before, she has the right outlook. Her turnover has already trebled this year. She is prepared to work and make something of it. She loves it.

However, the normal pattern is for married women to withdraw from the business as it expands. With the growth of the enterprise, the business owner concentrates on administration himself and hires people to do the work previously done by his wife who is left free either to pursue a career or to become a 'full-time' housewife. Usually, she becomes the latter. But if the wives of owner-controllers and owner-directors are less directly involved in working for the business, there is a tendency for them symbolically to represent the family *and* the company through a wide range of activities. These can involve the entertaining of potential customers, the maintenance of company 'morale' and participation in a number of locally-based associations. These points were aptly illustrated in the comments of Brian Logan, an owner-director, running a business with a £20 million turnover. At this size the company 'image' becomes important and wives are expected to promote it,

> I think that it is right that any business should have an involvement in the local community. I feel that quite strongly. My wife, for example, is fairly heavily involved in the community. So, to a fair

extent, she's involved in the business. I don't regard that as part of our private life. I regard it as part of our business life. The fact that it spills over till ten o'clock at night a couple of evenings a week is immaterial.

Indeed, the extent of female involvement in companies is such that grandmothers as well as wives often fulfil important symbolic roles. As another owner-director explained,

Grandmother is still very important in the business. She comes to every board meeting and attends every social function — and it's social functions which are so important. She only comes to board meetings so that when she goes to a social function she knows what's going on and can ask people about the job. We've something being finished right now and I've asked the manager to let me know when it's ready to be seen by grandmother so she can walk round and say 'How nice'. So again, people feel the family are involved. It's little things like that.

Clearly, then, even though married women may no longer fulfil productive functions in the larger companies, their involvement remains important. As we suggested earlier in this chapter, for the small business-man family and business relationships are always closely interrelated. Indeed, the fate of the one is intertwined with that of the other. Nowhere is this better demonstrated than in the problem of succession and bringing children into the business.[2] By definition, the family business is organised primarily for the benefit of the family. If the business has a legal form it is usually a private 'close' company with shares held tightly within the family.[3] But to ensure that the business stays in the family, competent children (and in our society that usually means sons) have to be produced — and produced at the right time. The absence of children can often reduce the owner's commitment to his business. As Roger Sims for example, confessed,

I've always had a good income — a good living from the firm. But having got plenty of money and not having a family, I've never let business be my boss. I've always taken a leisurely attitude towards business. If I had two or three children there would be something to work for but the wife can't have any children, and so it really boils down to the fact that we've nothing to work for — nothing to pass on.

But even if children are actually produced, 'timing' is always important if ownership and control are to be successfully passed on. This point was emphasised by Brian Logan, an owner-director,

> There are so many problems associated with succession. There's differences in ages, for example. You've got fathers of 40 and sons of 20 and that's quite a different situation from fathers of 40 and sons of 2 – entirely different. You shouldn't have very young people running fairly large businesses. You can have very young people involved but to bring them in straightaway to run the business is very often an absolute disaster.

Similarly, a small employer claimed,

> By the time my son is ready to come into the business – say in another five years when he's eighteen, I shall be 55. He wouldn't have any idea of what it's all about because the business isn't big enough for him to initially get in on the office side or anything like that. He wouldn't have the experience of running jobs. The pity about it is that we had our children too late. Now if he was between 20 and 24 it would be better but as it is, there's not going to be enough time. When I want to get out of it, he may not be ready to come into it.

Bringing a son into the business too early, or when he is simply incompetent, can cause serious problems, as the senior manager of a £12 million company stressed,

> If you've got the right person from the family in the right position, it's a good situation to be in. If you've got the wrong person, then life can be troublesome. Previously, this happened with other members of the family. They were brought into the business in places of responsibility just because they happened to be part of the family. This is where the family business falls flat on its face – it's a recipe for disaster. We're well clear of that now, thank goodness.

Assuming, however, that there are sons who are both willing and able to come into the family business, certain well-established procedures tend to be adopted. We found that fathers are determined that their sons should also 'work their way up', not necessarily on their own, but through *sponsored* mobility. Typically, the son first works for another company or companies before joining the father's business and he then gains further experience at different levels before being given a responsible position and ultimately taking over control from his father. The father then goes into semi- or full-time retirement but often continues to give advice and exercise influence 'behind the scenes'. He does this not only in his capacity as founder and former controller, but as a continuing shareholder.

The need for outside experience was emphasised by a small employer, Dick Crook, who claimed,

> I don't think it's good for children to come and work for their fathers, without having any other outside experience first. It's unfair because you're still treating them as children, although not intentionally. They should get a wider experience and know what it's like to work for somebody — what's expected of them and the working conditions. It's so easy to come straight into the business from home and it doesn't give them any wider experience of life at all.

Similarly, an owner-controller argued,

> I don't think children ought to be allowed into their father's business until they are about 35 years old — until they've been booted around the world a bit. I don't think 35 is a definite age, but until they've had a good 10, if not 15, years' experience of how to look after themselves rather than being brought into the fold and looked after by the father.

The continuing influence of the father was evident in two of the companies we studied, where the founder-owners were in the process of passing control to their sons. One owner-director, with a £6 million turnover, for example, had decided not to retire until he felt his sons were competent to take over,

> If I hadn't had sons there would have come a stage when I wouldn't have wanted to carry on anymore. It would have been a tragedy but it's terribly difficult to find a senior person, who's not a member of the family, who would give it the same attention. Colin was the first to come in and then Andrew. I've been terribly lucky because some sons would have pushed you around but they've been terribly good. Over the last five or six years I have slowly come out of it. It's all been worked out — they've done a tremendous amount of

work seeing how the firm should go and they've kept me in the picture about it. I can't disagree with anything they've done and it's working very well. Without them, I would have had to drop all my outside interests and there would have come a stage when I would have had to sell the business.

However, the continuing influence of the founder in the running of this particular business was emphasised by the company secretary,

> In the old days, the owner used to make a point of making himself known to everyone in the company from top to bottom. Then, the son took over and took some of the work off his father. The father then became Chairman and although he possibly doesn't come in that often he has his finger right on the pulse. They confer between themselves very much.

There comes a time, of course, when the founder has to leave the son completely in command. In this case, the company secretary had begun to notice a change in the style of leadership as the transition occurred,

> When the son came in I must say that the company really grew in strength profitability-wise. He began to engage middle management to take some of the responsibility. This made him slightly aloof – he didn't have the direct contact with the operatives because middle management was now absorbing this work. He didn't get involved in the detail to the same extent as his father.

The style changes, then, and there is a tendency for the son to be less autocratic than the father. Ths more egalitarian approach was reiterated by a senior manager in an owner-director's company,

> Before the son took over, his father Dereck was here and it was a different company entirely. This was mainly because he was loath to let anything out of his sight and this is one of the disadvantages of a family company. It all depends on the owner. Now with the son, the system and attitude we have is no different to that in any other type of company. He just appears like everybody else really. He has tried to produce this team spirit right the way through to the operatives – he has tried to make them all feel on a level footing. So his ideas on how the company should run are completely different from his father.

Clearly, when sons take over there are changes in the way in which the business is organised and this can generate considerable tension. From the son's point of view there is often an awareness that others may object to his sponsored advancement and feel that he is less then competent. The pattern of giving sons experience in other companies and at different levels within the family business is one of the major procedures whereby this tension can be resolved. But this is often not enough; sons are still seen to be favoured and this has implications for the ambitions and career patterns of senior managers. The problem is made worse when several family members are brought into the firm, as one owner-director recognised,

I have seen it happen many times, when you get too many of the family in the business. I would certainly fight against it. I've got three sons and it would be a disaster if they all wanted to be in it. I would hope that only one will probably come in. You can have too many family and then the other people have got no chance really. Too many of the family in the business is a disaster.

This point was more forcibly stated by Paul Ewing, the owner-controller of a group of companies with £1½ million annual turnover,

There's a tendency for those running family companies to think that they're never going to die or get decrepit and they seem to have a fear of bringing in 'new life'. So a lot of people in family businesses think there's never going to be any room for advancement. Family businesses tend to keep out outsiders, especially at Board level. So senior managers will go somewhere else where there's a chance of becoming a director.

However, by no means all business owners are determined to pass the business on to their sons. On the contrary, we found that a large number are not over-concerned about the long-term future of the business but rather with the transmission of their wealth and assets. Thus, many owners make every effort to enable their children to acquire capital which can then be used for entrepreneurial activities in a variety of business areas. Fathers tend to be keen for their children to continue the tradition of 'entrepreneurship' and to extend the family's assets in preference to the pursuit of careers within large-scale bureaucratic organisations. In a sense, this is a further reflection of the reluctance of entrepreneurial families to accept the constraints of working for others. A small employer for example, claimed,

> I don't think I would want my son to come in with me – not in this
> particular business. I don't know what he will do. He's trying to get
> an interest in the business but I'm doing my best to keep him out of
> it. But I would like both my son and daughter to run their own
> businesses. Then they can choose their own way of life . . . When
> you work for yourself you have more self-respect.

The concern to pass on assets within the entrepreneurial family can
be jeopardised, however, by quarrels and disputes. If, for example,
husband and wife are the major shareholders, a divorce can threaten
the future of a company in a similar manner as a dispute among shareholding brothers. In the latter instance, difficulties can sometimes be
resolved by the creation of 'separate' businesses, operating under the
general umbrella of the family holding company, within which family
members can pursue their interests in a more independent manner. In
other cases, however, such conflicts may encourage a son or a brother
to realise his assets and 'start again'. Some of these problems were illustrated for us by Paul Ewing,

> The company split right through the middle about three years ago.
> It was due, basically, to family differences. It's difficult to identify
> one particular reason but one side of the family didn't think too
> much of the capabilities of the other. That puts it in a nutshell and
> we, from our side, said it wasn't going to work in the future and so
> the best thing we could do was to split so we could go our own ways
> and have no axes to grind.

This brings us to our final point concerning the influence of personal factors in the long-term persistence of family businesses. In addition to 'suitable' children and the absence of family disputes, the
enthusiasm of actively involved family members is important. Even in
the larger businesses we found that the personality of the proprietor
permeated the whole company. In this sense, the 'health', 'age' and
'vitality' of owners is important. An executive director, for example,
claimed,

> A few years ago the owner was fired with enthusiasm and energy
> and he was breaking out into all sorts of different avenues and
> aspects – and taking the company with him. Unfortunately, a lot

of these didn't come to fruition and I think this must have had some effect on him because we're back now to the original company structure.

Naturally, 'self-made' men who are at or beyond retirement age tend to be less 'fired with enthusiasm' than some of their younger counterparts. One small employer, for example, could foresee no possibility of expansion in the business until 'the younger element root out the old boys like myself and my partner'. Similarly, Harold Doyle explained his refusal to expand — despite a considerable demand for his services — in the following terms, 'It just wouldn't be worthwhile. There'd be more money worries, more trouble, more wages to find every week, more office staff and all the rest. *No, not at my age* — I just don't want those sort of problems.' Given that Doyle was, at the age of 71 and without children, running single-handed a business which employed ten men, these sentiments are understandable. Nevertheless, they serve to emphasise that the vitality of small, private companies frequently reflects the variable capabilities of the founders, and often their families. Family and business cycles, then, are closely interconnected in a way which is unusual in larger corporate enterprises where organisational performance is less affected by the personalities of particular individuals.

Turning to styles of life we found that, in general, the proprietors we interviewed live rather modestly, primarily because they give priority to the business. The level of salary they pay themselves is clearly linked to the size of the business and to personal tax circumstances. Thus, among the owners of the largest enterprises we found that salaries are rarely above £15,000 a year while among the smaller employers £6,000 to £7,000 is typical. Although dividend payments are negligible, almost all of the owner-controllers and owner-directors supplement their income with fringe benefits such as private health insurance, expense accounts and company cars which are taxed, insured and fuelled by their businesses. Consequently, they are able to enjoy a material standard of living which is concealed behind a low, formal income and considerably above that of employees on a comparable level of earnings. But even so, their standard of living is not unusually high and it can best be described as 'lower middle-class' for the owners of the smaller enterprises and 'upper middle-class' for the owners of the larger concerns.

The 'lower middle-class' owners tend to live in three- or four-bedroomed detached houses. Furnishings are functional rather than decorative; kitchens, for example, are often full of the latest labour-saving devices, perhaps reflecting the extent to which women are necessarily drawn into running these smaller enterprises. Among the 'upper middle-class' owners of the larger enterprises, styles of living are rather more luxurious but less so than might be expected. By contrast with the owners of the smaller businesses, there is a tendency for children to attend fee-paying schools, for holidays to be taken abroad and for social events to be held in the home. The houses are larger, with five and six bedrooms, and set in sizeable, secluded gardens. They are filled with modern furniture with the occasional room used entirely as a bar. If the homes of the owners of smaller buisnesses are regarded as a retreat from work, these larger houses are presented as symbols of business success and personal achievement. Yet a rather ascetic attitude prevails which seems to be partly a function of their business experience. As George Arthur stated,

> You create the sort of environment in your working hours in which you think of ways of making money and saving money. Particularly, saving money. It's a bit like a colander. If you're going to be successful you've got to stop up the holes and stop the water pouring out everywhere in order to make it profitable. And if you're doing that all day, it flows over into your personal life.

In a similar manner, Stan Holdoway regretted that his employer did not spend more money on 'conspicuous consumption'. To do so, he felt, would be to the positive advantage of the company. As he suggested,

> The owner tries to play down the fact that he occasionally takes off on Friday to go horse-riding. But I think that those in the company should be pleased he can afford a £30,000 stable. That's the strange thing about him — he doesn't like to have a big flashy car or a country manor house. He lives extremely modestly which is a shame because when you get into the big company field, competing for jobs, these things matter. Other chairmen may turn their noses down at Brian Logan's house, this is the problem. It's the result of this puritanical streak. It was necessary in the early stages when we were very small but now there's no need for it.

While at the early stage of business growth it is necessary to invest rather than spend, at a later phase, it is important to 'be seen to spend' in order to advertise the success of the company. However, as Stan Holdoway's comments suggest, it is often difficult for many business owners to change their behaviour; as a result of their business activities they are investors rather than consumers. Indeed, even high consumption in the form of the ownership of large houses is often justified by reference to the investment opportunities they represent.

With few exceptions, most of the people we interviewed are 'satisfied' with their standard of living. This is not surprising since, as we have already suggested, they generally *choose* to squeeze personal consumption in preference for investment. If they do have any complaint about their economic circumstances, it is often in terms of low profit levels and the extent to which this affects business growth; in other words, it is a concern for re-investment rather than consumption. Further, they are little bothered with 'keeping up with the Joneses' and indeed 'the Joneses' do not even exist. As a self-employed proprietor stated,

I don't compare myself to anybody. I consider that we have a satisfactory standard of living. My wife doesn't go short of a great deal although, obviously, she may like a fur coat or that sort of thing. But we do go out in the evening for meals and things like that, and that's about all we expect. We don't expect Caribbean cruises — we're easily satisfied.

Similarly, another self-employed respondent claimed,

I'm not the type that worries about other people. Perhaps I'm a bit cocky because I'm in an ideal position. A lot of people would like it, I know. I've got everything I want here. I've got a family, no worries of a mortgage or anything like that and I'm living in the middle of an orchard and garden which is also my hobby. I'm quite happy with my returns — my standard of living is as good as anybody's.

We found that most of the people we talked with are quite unable to compare their living standards with other occupational groups in society. They often see themselves outside any clearly-defined class structure or status system.[4] As one owner-controller, for example, said,

I don't think I've ever compared myself to other groups. That sort of thing doesn't worry me. Over the years I've come to feel that I'm not in a class at all. I'm just myself and that's it. I know that a lot of people do concern themselves with these comparisons but it doesn't worry me.

For many, 'life' consists not of groups, categories and classes but of *individuals* which is perhaps to be expected in view of their own individualistic personal careers. Consequently, they can neither compare nor identify with managers, professional workers and other groups in general. If any comparisons are made for evaluating consumption patterns, they tend to be *historical* in terms of their own personal experience. As a small employer told us,

I've never made comparisons because I'm not interested in how anybody else goes on. We don't bother with what other people have got. We're quite happy in our own way, thank you. We don't ask for too much — we feel that just living here is Shangri-La compared with where we used to live. So, compared with the past, no one can deny we are much better off. I was pretty ambitious when I was younger. I used to be worried about whether the business was going wrong and how it could be improved. I'm not going to say that ambition has been thrown out of the window but I'm contented with my lot.

A similar point was made by another small employer,

When it comes down to brass tacks you can only sleep in one bed, you can only have three meals a day and you don't need any more. Once you start getting away from that, then it becomes what I call, 'airy-fairy' and ethereal. I've experienced life at its worst. I was a prisoner of war and then, the first thing you think about is keeping alive, the second thing is keeping warm and the third, is eating enough food. These are the three basics and that's what life is all about. Everything else, apart from that, in my opinion is all superfluous to life.

The absence of any comparative groups for the purposes of assessing notions of personal well-being is reinforced by the existence of a private and family-centred way of life. There are those who are highly involved in a wide range of community-based activities and associations and, as we have already suggested, these can have beneficial 'spin-off' effects for the business. There are others, however, who are committed to various organisations and associations for totally 'non-business' reasons. But on the whole, these are exceptional; the general pattern is for very limited participation. The owner-director of a large company was fairly typical when he stated,

I've been invited to join various clubs and societies – Round Table and Rotary and what have you. I've never done so because I've always felt that the business has got to come first. If I'm fully involved with the business I haven't got time for these other things. I've also got a family and I want to spend as much time as I can with them.

A rejection of social involvement in preference for more home-centred activities was stressed by an owner-controller,

I don't 'belong' if you know what I mean. I've had chances to join the Masons and all that sort of thing, but I haven't because in the end, it takes charge of you and you have no time at all. I keep my leisure time entirely private. When I sometimes go to functions I find that you finish up 'talking shop' the whole evening. There's nothing I hate more than that. So I stay at home a lot with my family and my garden – that's all.

Business owners, then, tend to lead very private lives. Part of the explanation for this is their rather atypical work experience. Instead of acquiring educational qualifications and embarking upon careers within bureaucratic structures they have 'done it their way'. Consequently, their formal educational qualifications are limited and they are often extremely conscious of this. As Eddie Lawrence, a wealthy owner-controller stated,

I never deal with the paper-work side of the business because of my educational standards, you see . . . I didn't have a proper education . . . I've just put my son into a private school . . . because I'd rather him not suffer that burden. I can afford it and so why not. I just hope he doesn't get too intelligent and drifts away and thinks that his father is illiterate.

Eddie Lawrence, then, although highly successful in making money, is very aware of his limited educational background which clearly curtails his willingness to socialise. This is further reinforced by the lack of time because of the priority given to the business. Indeed, because they devote so much of their lives to business many owners have virtually no time for anything else. As a result, they seem to lose the skill to cultivate extended social relationships. Overwhelmingly, devotion to the business entails the sacrifice of almost everything else. Indeed, social marginality tends to be a *consequence* rather than a *cause* of business growth.[5] The greater majority of the people that we interviewed came from relatively poor working-class backgrounds. However, *without* educational qualifications but *with* the growth of their enterprises they had become 'middle class' in their material living standard. Consequently, they now see themselves as marginal to, and 'outside' of, the class structure; as too affuent to be 'working class' but lacking in the cultural skills necessary to be completely 'middle class'. This ambiguity and its implications for personal life-style was summed up by Harold Doyle, a small employer,

> I'm still working-class in a sense — perhaps a little bit up from the bottom. But then there's speech, there's accent and then there's other different things that always give the game away to people who know. You often wonder, no matter how much money you had, whether you'd ever be quite so 'nice' as what they are. This is the difference. But it's never bothered me. I've never had time for 'social life'. When I go home, I want to go home to a fire, an armchair and a paper or a good book, that's all I want. I don't want to go out for drinks or to parties.

But the consequences can be more far-reaching, especially for those who completely devote their lives to the expansion of their enterprises and subsequently become extremely wealthy. For them, there is often a crisis of personal identity and a tendency for self-appraisal which leads to a re-assessment of the rewards of making money. This was reflected in the opinions of Eddie Lawrence,

> Money creates materialistic things, but the more materialistic things you get the less valuable they are . . . If I find something I want I get it. I don't particularly want it but I've got it. You mentioned the swimming pool. You haven't got one. You'd love to have one. But if you've got one it doesn't mean that much . . . I really don't know whether I'm satisfied or not. My basic ambition was to earn a lot of money quickly and retire. But during the time you're earning the money you're so involved that you don't develop any hobbies to speak of. Then when you arrive at the level you thought you wanted to stop at you suddenly realise, 'Well, what do I do now?'

There are, then, heavy social and personal costs borne by the 'self-made' man and his family. Married women in particular, and the family in general, provide a hidden but necessary investment during the initial stages of the business. Further, family life continues to suffer as the business grows because family and business are intricately interconnected. The entrepreneurial family, then, is distinct from other family forms in that its relationships can effect the long-term prospects of the business enterprise. For most people, by contrast, work and family relationships are kept quite separate. But are the costs worthwhile? This is something which only the individuals, themselves, can decide. Certainly, some of the proprietors we interviewed make conscious decisions to stop at various stages of business growth if only because the costs for personal satisfaction, life-styles and social relationships are too much. Others, however, achieve considerable business 'success' only to then be subject to severe self-doubts about their personal competence and the meaning of their lives. Nevertheless, society regards such men as highly successful. But how do they regard society? This is the subject for the next two chapters.

Notes

1. For a discussion of family life among salaried managers, see J.M. and R.E. Pahl, *Managers and their Wives* (Harmondsworth, 1971).

2. For a detailed analysis of family succession in small businesses see, J. Boswell, *The Rise and Decline of Small Firms* (London, 1973).

3. A discussion of legal forms can be found in M. Chesterman, *Small Businesses* (London, 1977).

4. For a discussion of the ways in which small business owners regard themselves as 'outside' the class structure see, F. Bechhofer, B. Elliott, M. Rushforth and R. Bland, 'The Petits Bourgeois in the Class Structure: The Case of the Small Shopkeepers' in F. Parkin (ed.), *The Social Analysis of Class Structure* (London, 1974).

5. Thus, the relationship between entrepreneurship and social marginality is often quite the reverse to that frequently suggested in sociological explanations of business owners' behaviour.

8 WHAT'S WRONG WITH BRITAIN? BUSINESS OWNERS' ATTITUDES ON THE STATE AND ECONOMY

In the opening chapter we looked at the current enthusiasm for the small businessman. We tried to explain why politicians regard small businesses as the basis for the economic regeneration of British society. In this and the following chapter we reverse the emphasis in order to describe the way in which business proprietors view the society in which they live. Of course, there are always difficulties in trying to summarise the attitudes of people because their ideas and opinions are often changeable and contradictory. Furthermore, the interviewing process can generate attitudes which did not previously exist. Nevertheless, with certain limitations, it is possible to present a fairly accurate picture of how small businessmen perceive their socio-political environment.

It is perhaps important to stress that the interviews took place during the autumn of 1979. This followed the election of a Conservative Government committed to re-creating the conditions in which small businesses can flourish. It is likely that political statements in the media helped shape opinions that were previously ill-formed and almost certainly encouraged the expression of opinions that might otherwise have been regarded as inappropriate. However, it is necessary to bear in mind that attitudes are not solely derived from the media but are also formed through concrete personal experiences. Sometimes these reinforce each other while on other occasions they are the basis for considerable uncertainty and ambiguity.

As might be expected, the strongest personal belief is in the virtues of the market both as an economic system and as a guarantor of individual rights and freedoms. Most feel that if modern society is in decline it is because social change is making it increasingly difficult for individuals to achieve the promises of liberal democracy. The collectivism of the state and trade unionism, combined, is eroding the freedom and liberty of the individual. Indeed, the political parties, trade unions and the state are all seen as integral and inseparable parts of a package which is undermining the essential tenets of Western democracy.[1] One owner-director expressed this attitude vigorously,

I get the shudders sometimes at some of the things which are said by our politicians which could very well lead us on the road to the Stalinist state. I must say I don't like the smell of it at all. I get a bit wary when we begin to breach some of the fundamentals of democracy. This is what I would fight to the last ditch – this attempt to deny the right of free speech, to say what you think. We still have our elections and we still have a free press. But I get worried when I hear Michael Foot giving a speech in favour of the closed shop. If you are going to say that a trade union can decide whether, for example, an editor of a newspaper can work or not, then I get worried. The same applies to any attempt to restrict parliamentary democracy. It's a question of balance which we have to work out for ourselves. We are never going to reach the perfectly fair society, which equally serves free enterprise on the one hand and the bottom of the heap, socially, on the other. A friend of mine doesn't think it is right that radio discjockeys should earn £50,000 a year. But how do you reckon what a man's worth? If you believe in a free enterprise economy, they are worth what the public will pay. We are beginning now, as a result of the Conservative victory in the last election, to question whether we really should have a change of course.

In this view things are going wrong because the state and trade unions have become too powerful. Others referred to the state as 'Big Brother', 'parasitic' and 'corrosive' and often regarded it as a consequence of Labour Government and trade-union inspired legislation which has curtailed the 'freedom' of the individual. Employment legislation, for example, is seen to be a fundamental attack upon the prerogatives of individual employers. As an owner-director stated,

> The Employment Protection legislation and all the other jungle of paper-work and problems which we have are unnecessary. I think the government should leave us alone and let us get on with it – to hire and fire and resolve these things ourselves.

But it goes further than this. 'Big Brother' is also seen to regulate everyday life in an ever-more pervasive fashion. As Desmond Reid told us,

> There must be opportunity for people to use their own initiative. It's not just a matter of money and taxes but a matter of satisfaction in life. Everything that takes away from the individual the ability to do what he thinks best and to use his resources in the way he thinks is

best for him, his family and those he is responsible for – the more this is taken away and made the responsibility of Big Brother – the more the possibility of personal growth is inhibited.

The state, then, is seen to be increasingly powerful. But at the same time it is regarded as 'parasitic'; a number of proprietors argued that the state is unproductive and inefficient, living off the rest of society. It is often because of this that taxes are resented – they enable an unproductive bureaucracy to impose unnecessary and 'totalitarian' legislative measures. This point was bluntly expressed by an owner-controller: 'It's ridiculous. What we've really done is to create a new type of class, haven't we? The parasites in our government offices.' A similar point was made by Roger Sims who stated,

We keep paying taxes and employing people in government offices who are getting lots of money for doing next to nothing except for a lot of unnecessary paperwork. I certainly don't want to pay a lot of taxes to keep a load of dumb wits in employment.

In addition, the state is wasteful. As Howard Crompton argued,

I'm in favour of decent social services and good hospital services but I'm not in favour of the way these things are run. An awful lot of money is just wasted. Obviously government must run these thing but there are just too many unproductive administrators.

It would, then, be wrong to infer that small businesses are completely opposed to *all* state activities; many feel that not enough is being spent on education and the social services. It is more a question of keeping the state out of certain activities, especially its *direct* and *indirect* involvement in the country's industrial production. Thus, the nationalised industries are regarded as big spenders, relying upon taxpayers to 'bail them out' and to provide them with unlimited financial resources. As Keith Deane, an owner-controller, claimed,

I honestly think that if a lot of businesses were totally left to private enterprise, they would either go to the wall or they would look for alternatives. A private business, be it large or small, does not have a bottomless pit. The shipbuilding industry, for example, is going to cost a fortune before we know where we are. If it had been left in private hands they would have gone broke. British Leyland – they went to the government and asked for x million pounds or else they'd wrap up. But they wouldn't have wrapped up; they would have hived off bits of it which, by now, would have developed into other businesses.

In other words, economic production should be completely left to privately-owned enterprises whose success (or failure) should be determined by market forces. But *indirect* state intervention is also resented because it obliges enterprises to undertake many 'unproductive' activities such as the completion of government returns. As Desmond Reid stated,

> There's an enormous amount of work that is necessary to produce statutory returns which are set out in a format that pays no regard to the kind of records kept within a company. On the legislation side, we have to digest a continually changing volume of laws. You hardly have time to sort out one set before another piles on top of it. An executive who really tries to do his job has far too much of his time spent on 'negative' work. In fact, we've got a kind of mini civil-service within our company doing what the government imposes upon us. Recently, employment protection has caused us to spend a lot of time taking staff away from jobs for internal training just in order that they should not put a foot wrong and land us in an Industrial Tribunal.

The state is also regarded as 'corrosive' since it undermines traditional attitudes towards work. Social welfare, it is claimed, accounts for the decline of Britain as an industrial nation, because it is no longer worthwhile for many people to work. This was repeatedly emphasised by owners, irrespective of the size of their enterprise. Roger Sims, for example, argued,

> There's too much social security — that's basically what's wrong with the country. Too many people can get too much easy money. I'm not talking about disabled people, I think they should be treated in a completely different way. But an ordinary person, if he's out of work, should be made to sweep the roads, cut the hedges and give them just sufficient for a loaf of bread. Until that time arrives, we're never going to get people to work properly. Why should they work for £60 a week when they can get £50 for doing nothing?

In a similar vein, an owner-controller stated,

All these people who are out of work — no one seems to realise they don't want to work. Mrs Thatcher's idea of making the dole money further away from the average wage packet is a very good idea because that will make them work. But when a chap can go on the dole and get £47 a week tax free and then do a couple of evenings in the pub and get that tax free, what's the point of working and paying income tax?

This owner referred not only to unemployment benefits but also to the operation of a 'black' economy which, together, are destroying incentives to work. The consequence is the creation of an 'unemployable' sector of society. According to an owner-director,

That 1½ million unemployed — or whatever it is — are unemployable. They don't intend to work. You see when I get short I contact the labour exchange and I can guarantee what they send me for interview is not worth employing. If I do start them, they won't last more than a week or two, or else they will be making trouble.

Making a related point, self-employed Mel Morgan claimed,

I can give you the local paper and there's a bloody page full of jobs, yet there's so many thousand unemployed and on the dole round here. I mean, I don't care what it is — I'd sweep the roads if I had to. There's always a job. If you want a job you can go out and find one. You'll get one if you want one. But all I can say is, there must be a lot of people who just don't want work.

The development of the welfare state, then, is seen to have affected attitudes towards getting work. But it is also considered to have important consequences for behaviour *at work*. As an executive director in one of the larger companies suggested, there has been a decline in discipline and authority in the workplace because legislative changes and developments in the educational system have made workers less inclined to carry out orders,

Schooling habits have changed over the past decade when strict discipline was very much the order of the day. You had to work very hard at school, then when you left, it was the same pace at work —

there was a strict discipline there as well. I know as a lad I was driven very hard indeed but it was to my benefit in the long term. These days people don't work so hard – in the south, at least, there are more jobs available and it's also partly the employer's fault because we've not maintained the discipline over the years. We've lost it, what with all this employment legislation which has tended to have quite an effect on the lack of discipline at work.

This point was further emphasised by an owner-controller who also saw a clear relationship between present-day schooling and a decline in work attitudes,

I think that basically our whole educational system has to be reviewed. Everybody has got to be re-educated. There's no discipline taught in schools. We've really got to get down to basics and the main fundamentals. People just don't want to work hard any more.

But the fault is not only a lack of discipline in schools. According to some businessmen, people have become 'over-educated' and this makes them less willing to accept managerial prerogatives. A self-employed proprietor, for example, told us,

You get more conflict as people get more educated and become more aware. The uneducated person has always been taken advantage of so perhaps with more educated people you'll get more discontent. With this improvement of education over the last couple of generations, people are more aware that they are being taken advantage of by employers – this is what it amounts to.

In a sense, this is a neat summary of the way in which social change has affected the employment relationship in modern society. Among other things, changes in the educational system have broken down paternalism and the deferential order, and replaced them with a greater emphasis upon democratic personal relationships which, in many ways, create tensions in the management and organisation of labour. The employers, then, blame the schools for managerial problems in the workplace. If schools would only instil children with self-discipline, they would later be able to control them *as workers* much more easily. But if the state fails to produce people equipped with the *general* capabilities to be 'good' employees, it is also incapable of giving potential workers *particular* skills through, for example, industrial retraining schemes. As an owner-director stated,

> As far as job-retraining is concerned, it's hopeless. They think they are teaching them the right things but they are not teaching them anything. And the sad thing is, that these people come out of re-training centres thinking they know everything and when they get to work, they find that they know nothing.

It seems as though the state can't win, even when it tries explicitly to meet the requirements of business! However, it may be more than this; possibly the problem is that the state gives workers skills which enable them to be less attached to specific employers and, thus, more mobile in the labour market. When, on the other hand, the employer does the training, it is often *specific* to his own particular needs and, further, commits the worker both technically and morally.

The state, then, is regarded as 'Big Brother', 'parasitic' and 'corrosive'. It is part of a package that is seen to be preventing businessmen from getting on with the job. A further important component is trade unionism, either in conjunction with the state or in isolation. Many employers, in *principle*, are not opposed to trade unionism which they regard as fulfilling important functions. But, in *practice*, they argue that unions are too powerful and abuse their position in society. However, there were few trade union members in the companies we studied and employers usually prefaced their remarks by claiming that unions were of little immediate importance. Their opinions, then, were received and interpreted from secondary sources and, unlike their general comments about the role of the state, they were unable to illustrate these with specific examples of actual practices. Overall, there is a widespread lack of direct contact with trade unions in this sector and small business owners are anxious to keep it that way. As Paul Ewing said,

> Generally speaking, I think the unions have a lot to answer for — particularly their pig-headed attitudes towards modernisation which certainly impedes progress. Personally, as far as our company is concerned, we are not very involved with unions, I am thankful to say. I must admit, if we were, we would pack up. I'm not joking, I think we as a family would get out. We wouldn't tolerate it. I'm not messing around — I feel that strongly about it. If we deal with people, we deal with them — I would say — as master and servant. They can say what they like, you can say what you like. And that's it.

For many owners there was a romantic age of trade unionism when they knew their place in society and, because of the ruthlessness of some employers, there were things to be fought for. Now that workers have gained fundamental legal and social rights, the essential purpose of trade unionism has been fulfilled. As a small employer claimed,

> Let's go back to the early days before the war. Things weren't very happy then. People couldn't join unions just as they liked. I've worked for a firm myself that said definitely no unions. But the unions did do a lot of good things for men. They bought the standard of living up to what it is today. Without them, it would still be 'Yes sir, no sir, three bags full sir' to the governors. The unions did more for this country and for working men than anybody can realise. The trouble is, they've swung to a political bias now.

Many of the employers we interviewed come from manual working-class backgrounds and this encourages a strong attachment to the principle of trade unionism, even though their perception of current practices is generally negative. This is evident in Keith Large's remarks,

> I don't have anything against trade unions. They've done a fantastic amount of good in their own way. As I say, I had a strong socialist upbringing — my father was a miner and he has told me at length the situation in this country before there were trade unions and before unions were able to negotiate decent wages and conditions for employees. But the point is, they should confine themselves to that — they should not enter into politics. I do not accept, however strongly a union feels, that they have the right to interfere by, say, imposing sanctions on countries like South Africa. They're over-stepping their authority when they involve people who are not members of their own particular union. When they start to interfere with other unions and other businesses, this is all wrong.

Trade unions, then, should not engage in 'politics'. But even within the industrial sphere, all is not well. Unions are seen to cultivate inefficiency, idleness and the expectation among workers that they should get something for nothing. In this respect, they reinforce the 'corrosive' influence of the welfare state. One owner-controller, for example, argued,

> There is a place for unions — I don't think they ought to be abol-

ished. What I am saying is that they should keep a sense of proportion. They shouldn't regard profits as a dirty word. Just because Ford made a profit they think it's terrible. And when it comes to them all going on strike just because they haven't got enough sugar in their tea, well then, it's really gone full circle hasn't it?

Trade unions also cultivate economic inefficiency because they are seen to restrict labour mobility. As Charles Thorpe claimed,

I don't like any trade unions. I've always done a job which I liked and I've always been of a mind that if I didn't like the job I'd stop and do something else. I think trade unionists have the same opportunity. If they are not happy with the work they do why don't they get out of it and do something else instead of going on strike and stopping the bloody country. They can move can't they? Why stop in one place – blimey, the poor buggers walked from Jarrow didn't they years ago?

Further, they foster idleness. According to a small employer,

They've got out of hand haven't they? Now the cards are turned the other way. In my opinion, the attitude now is that if a man doesn't work he's considered to be a good chap. If he works hard, well he's seen to be a bloody idiot. This is the problem – I'd be bored to tears.

It is clear from these remarks that trade unions are frequently blamed for the country's industrial decline. Indeed, as part of a 'package' which includes the state and the political parties, they are viewed as *the* dominant force, it is the unions that rule the country rather than elected governments. As one owner-controller stated,

The unions make me sick. They tell the government what they can and cannot do. We elect a government to run the country – to govern. But the unions, who are just for one creed, they're telling the government what they can do. They even get the government to pay them to strike don't they?

Because trade unions 'rule' the country they are often seen to be above the 'law'. Harold Doyle, for example, argued,

The unions are using their power wrongly. But there again, it's not so much the unions I blame for what's happening but rather that the law is not standing up to them. The moment they think the unions are going to bring the men out, firms run away – and they run away because the law hasn't backed them up. If a man gets caught pinching things, they keep him on rather than have a strike on their hands. But if the law sent that bloke to prison for twelve months then things would be different. But no, law and order has fallen down in this country.

If the consort of trade unions, the state and the political parties is generally alien to the interests of business, it is only the Conservative Party which is seen to offer any kind of solution. On the whole, small businessmen feel politically under-represented and even their attachment to the Conservative Party is weaker than is commonly assumed. Nevertheless, the Conservatives are, for them, the only potential force likely to remedy the abuses of trade unionism and the welfare state. The general attitude was summed up by Barry Small, 'I'm Tory. I feel that if anything's going to be done for us it's going to come from that direction. But I really don't give out a lot of hope.' Indeed, we found there is a general cynicism towards politicians and the political system. At best they interfere with the effective operation of market forces and at worst they are incompetent and unproductive – 'living off' tax-payers' money and making little contribution to the nation's welfare. In this there is little to choose between the major political parties although, sometimes, the Liberal Party is considered more favourably because of its anti-bureaucratic image. Certainly, most cynicism is directed towards the Labour Party. Not only is it in the hands of the trade unions – as an owner-controller argued, 'the Labour Party shouldn't really be called the Labour Party, it should be called the Trade Union Party' – but its leadership is also seen to be more concerned to serve its own interests rather than those of rank-and-file supporters. Roger Sims, for example, suggested,

The Labour Party is supposed to be for the working man, but when you get people like Callaghan and Wilson who've got two or three houses and large farms, how can you call them working-men's people? They've made it. They've invested. They've all had their fingers in business earning a bit. They're capitalists the same as the rest of us, so they're sitting pretty.

Similarly, Mel Morgan stated,

> The Labour Party make me bloody sick. There's Wilson on tele-
> vision talking about housing – he's got three. One in the Isle of
> Scilly, one in Hampstead and one in Suffolk. All the buggers have
> got three apiece and they talk about housing. I haven't got time for
> any of them.

But most agree with Howard Crompton. He suggested there was little to
choose between the parties,

> When you really get down to brass tacks, I don't think the big polit-
> ical parties represent anybody in particular. I don't think the Con-
> servatives are particularly for Big Business or that the Labour Party
> go for the working man. I may be a bit cynical . . . It's interesting
> from a distance but I would never get worked up and become a
> party worker. I would like to see the Liberals gain a bit of influence,
> though. I think it's a very good thing to have a third party.

The ultimate expression of political disillusionment came from Harold
Doyle who echoed the frustration of many of our respondents,

> If I had a say, there'd be regular hours in the House of Commons.
> There'd be none of this midnight lark. They'd be there at nine in the
> morning and they wouldn't stop until five. There'd be no bars or
> beer in the House of Commons and the heat would be cut down to
> about 45°F. You've got 600 people, all the best about. Plenty of
> beer, whisky, meals and all the rest of it. Each one trying to be
> cleverer than the other. And then you wonder that you get bad laws
> and bad government! The atmosphere is absolutely right for it,
> isn't it? You just can't go on like that and govern a country!

Views of the political system are closely interrelated with opinions
about the organisation of society in general and the class structure in
particular. Most of the proprietors view social class in terms of life-
styles, patterns of consumption and social status. Given this, they
regard themselves as outside the class system because they are not
'snobs' and they 'treat everyone the same'. But with workers it is different. As an owner-controller emphasised,

> I think there's a class structure but, as usual, it's built upside down.

It's the workers that form it. Me — I can go out and meet anybody. We've got half a dozen lords and ladies on our books and I can go out and talk to them and it doesn't worry me. They're only human beings so you certainly don't need to go kotowing to them.

Perhaps more importantly, business owners estimate people according to their social contribution. As such, they generally categorise occupations in terms of whether they are productive and contribute to the nation's economic and social welfare. Generally speaking politicians, trade union officials, civil servants and all those in the state sector are seen as unproductive, while those engaged in economic and business activities in the private sector are regarded as productive. A finer distinction separates out employers and manual workers as productive but categorises most salaried office workers as an unproductive but necessary overhead in most enterprises. A small employer summed up the situation as follows,

All the artisans that work with their hands are worthy of a good amount of money. I don't honestly think that people in offices should earn anymore than they do. Those chaps that *really create* are better than the blokes that just aid. A chap like myself is the key to a business. This is not being big-headed. This is the bloke that counts. After that, it's the manual workers, the men that do the job. The skilled blokes. The chaps in the office, they're only aides. Any reasonably educated person can do that job, as long as there's someone at the top to tell them and there's men on the job to do the work. They're the two most important ones.

Office employees, then, may be necessary but they are generally unproductive. Further, an identification between the interests of employers and manual workers overrides any conflicts that surround the profit motive. Indeed, no such conflicts are considered to exist; employers *and* workers share a common interest in profits since these improve the living standards of *all*. If there are low wages — as many employers recognise — it is seen as a function of competition in the market, and hence, beyond their control.

On the face of it, there is a contradiction in the attitudes of employers towards trade unions and those towards productive workers; they are hostile to one but not the other. The explanation lies largely in the fact that these employers have a very limited personal experience of trade unionism. Their views on unions come from hearsay and the media's attention to 'militancy' and 'extremism' within the trade union movement.[2] This is thought to be quite unrelated to their own workers who 'just want to do a fair day's work for a fair day's pay'. Opinions of this sort were expressed by an owner-controller who told us,

> The apathy of the working man is something to be seen in order to be believed. In trade unions it's always the same half dozen who turn up at branch meetings and you always get more enthusiasm on your extreme left than you do on the right or the middle of the road. They are so dominated by the left-wing that workers don't want to know – so long as they get their wage increases. They don't attend the meetings and they don't vote. The general attitude is complete apathy.

Further, if conflict exists in the workplace, it is the trade unions' fault not the workers; they have been 'corrupted' by irresponsible unionism. As Roger Sims argued,

> Over the years, since companies have had to declare profits and the unions have started shouting for more money and asking why they should suffer at the expense of big companies, class distinctions have become a major factor. It was never a factor when I was a boy, even in the 1950s when I was an apprentice.

The notion of productive contribution clearly has important implications for attitudes towards wage differentials. Employers assume that they should receive high economic rewards because of the risks which they undertake, the employment they create and the production of goods and services which society needs. There is, therefore, no conflict between producing goods and services in order to make profits and contributing to the welfare of society; the two are closely associated. Dick Crook emphasised the need for profits as a reward for risks,

> At the top of the ladder ought to be the man who has put everything at risk – his house and everything financially. He's lived for a number of years, perhaps on a very low income, putting in massive hours and now he's made it. He's getting possibly £20,000 or £30,000 a year, lives in a nice big house and has got his business running successfully. That man deserves his high earnings because he has put everything on the line in order to get it.

According to Roger Sims,

> People don't stop to think that others are risking their capital in a
> firm to give people work. They don't stop and look at it that way. If
> I've got a thousand pounds and want to invest it somewhere, I ex-
> pect a return on it don't I?

A similar argument in favour of rewards for effort and personal sacrifice
leads to the support of claims for higher pay by productive manual
workers. Alec Stephens, an owner-controller, argued for this,

> I think people on assembly lines earn what they get because their
> jobs are boring and they are paid because of the lack of interest. So
> I suppose they're not well-paid – you've got to pay them just for the
> sheer boredom. I think that coalminers do deserve what they get.

As did a small employer,

> The miners, and all those that do that type of work, are underpaid.
> You wouldn't get me down a mine for less than £500 a week. I just
> couldn't do it. So, if you're talking about asking somebody to go
> down for £70 or £80 a week, I just couldn't ask them to do it.
> To my mind, they are underpaid for what they do.

Many employers feel that their own workers are underpaid, given the
conditions under which they work. However, market conditions and
the need to stay competitive mean that higher wages cannot be
afforded. Office workers, on the other hand, are regarded with some
suspicion and often considered to be overpaid. Roger Sims felt,

> People working in offices are grossly over-paid, I think, unless they
> are doing a specific job which is not routine – where they've got to
> use a lot of specialist knowledge. People who do basic office work
> are doing a very routine, mediocre job and there's no way that they
> can compare with a production worker. They are not really, half of
> them, doing anything.

Alec Stephens also stated,

> There's too many people working in suits and bowler hats as against
> people working – actually turning out the real work. There ought to

be more people doing that sort of job and less working in offices —
passing one piece of paper to another for the other person to deal
with. A lot of offices have sixteen people in them when eight would
do.

But these opinions are most strongly expressed over the earnings of
higher-paid civil servants and politicians. Mel Morgan spoke for many,

Some people get paid far more than what they are worth. MPs for
a start. Most of them say they work till ten at night. But if you go
into the House of Commons they're just sitting there and they're not
particularly bothered about what's going on anyway, are they?
They've just had a big pay rise — they seem to give themselves rises
but nobody else. Then all these nationalised industries, they are all
losing money because they've got too many chiefs and not enough
indians. There's too many people at the top earning £50,000 a year
and then all the little hangers-on earning £30,000 a year and then all
the little secretaries earning £15,000.

However, there are occupations in the public sector which make a social
contribution. These include nurses, doctors and teachers. Many
employers share a close affinity with these jobs because the production
of goods and the generation of profits are seen to be just as necessary
for the welfare of society as the more explicitly 'caring' occupations. In
other words, society needs entrepreneurs just as it needs medical services. A small employer, for example, felt,

People should be paid according to what they do for the community. Take a surgeon as an example, he really should be paid much
more than someone who sweeps the road. The surgeon and his
nursing staff — we totally rely on them — yet I think that sometimes
they get a raw deal.

Peter Rivard claimed,

Nurses should definitely have more money. If there were no nurses
you might as well shut down, that's the way I look at the country.
I mean to say, nursing is most essential. Well, then, why shouldn't
they get a good wage to keep them there and keep them happy —
the happier they are, the better they work.

Similarly, another small employer stated,

> I would put nurses and primary school teachers at the top of the earnings table. They just don't get enough out of it. Primary school teachers, in particular, do one of the most important jobs — far more important than many other occupations.

We have, then, briefly reviewed the business owners' views of the socio-political situation. It is derived from two sets of influences — the mass media and other secondary sources, and the personal experience of running businesses. Some attitudes are more firmly held then others and, within these, there are certain contradictions. However, the core judgement is clear. Producing goods for a profit is *the* major social contribution and ought to be the mainspring of modern society. Groups and institutions that are not part of this process are regarded as parasitic. This, indeed, is how they view the state, trade unions and the political parties since, at worst, they undermine and at best, they interfere with the efficient operation of this productive dynamic. Even the Conservative Party, which deliberately appeals to the interests of business proprietors, is regarded with some doubt and scepticism. As one of the self-employed told us,

> I feel that both the political parties are to blame — they're just no good in my opinion. I'm a Tory by necessity, if you know what I mean. It's the only chance that I've got to maintain my own situation, really. But it's no good a Tory candidate coming round to me and saying that they'll be backing the small businessmen because I would call him a liar on his past record.

Thus, the Tories are often seen as the agents of big business, another potentially corroding influence on Western society. While it is recognised that large-scale enterprises are inevitable because of the needs of modern markets and complex technological processes, they are also seen as a threat to small firms. This point was emphasised by an owner-controller,

> There really should be control of monopolies shouldn't there? If a firm has, say, twelve branches that should be the limit shouldn't it? No single business should be able to commandeer, for example, all the grocery trade in one area. One national firm said a year ago that it was going to cut prices and put all small shops out of busi-

ness. Why should these firms be forcing small firms out of business? Because once they have got a complete monopoly, they can do what they like. They can restrict the number of products on sale so that they only offer what they get most profit on. So if you are small you just can't compete and it would be futile to try.

Furthermore, big business is regarded as losing the essential characteristics of efficient, productive enterprises. As another owner-controller stated,

I think big business has had its day — I never did think very highly of it. People make the mistake of equating bigness with efficiency and ability. This is quite wrong. The only thing you can equate with big business is its ability to do big things, but I bet I use my money more efficiently than they do, I bet I use my staff more effectively than they do and I bet I use my labour to a greater effect as well. So if you want to calculate usefulness to society as a whole, small businesses are more useful in this sense than big ones.

In a similar manner, a self-employed proprietor claimed,

Big business and multiple groups have proved by their record that they don't work. In fact they, more than anything, have created the present economic crisis. I'm a great believer that they are a major cause of the unemployment situation, for example, because they deprive the smaller company of a living and then it turns out that they are unable to do the job any better. All they've done is to put firms of, perhaps, ten men *out* of work, put three thousand men *in* work for five years, and then put the whole three thousand *out* of work at the end of that period. So, from my point of view, one of the major factors is that the government has allowed the companies to become too big.

From these opinions, it is clear that small business owners feel themselves to be under attack. It's bad enough with the state and the trade unions, but when 'big business' is also undermining the economic system, the problems become severe! What, then, are the solutions?

Interestingly, owners turn to the government as the instrument of change and herein lies the major contradiction in their thinking. They want the importance of the state to be reduced and yet insist upon strong state action to get something done. The contradiction is partially resolved by a continuing belief in the Conservative Party. Despite considerable cynicism, there is hope that the Conservatives will free the state from its alliance with the trade unions, reduce its size and re-direct it towards serving the *real* needs of a market economy.[3] The state's main function should simply be to provide a framework within which private enterprise can operate according to the dictates of the market. At best, the state should only offer guidelines and stipulate minimum requirements – for example, in such areas as competition, wage levels, health and safety – and should make no attempt to prescribe and to dictate. A small employer put it succinctly,

> The government must create the right sort of climate for businesses. Businesses will look after themselves if they have got the right climate. The job of the government is to create the conditions under which businesses can mushroom.

But in order to bring this about, it is considered necessary to have a strong state free from the domination of the largely unrepresentative trade unions.

As part of this climate the state must also re-create feelings of national unity, foster traditional family values, stimulate a renewed commitment to hard work and self-sacrifice, and provide an economic environment within which smaller businesses can flourish. The need for leadership and a new sense of national purpose was frequently emphasised. A small employer was typical when he argued,

> I can't believe that this country is going to sink beyond all trace. We could do with a few more speeches by Sir Harold Macmillan to stir the country up. He's got that sort of power, Churchill had it. Sir Winston was a born leader of men, whether you agreed with him or not, he had the habit of making you do something. Now Macmillan made a very stirring speech before the last election [1979] and that was the sort of thing that Churchill did. When you've got your back against the wall, you really go for it.

In a similar fashion, an owner-controller stated,

> There's something in the British character that comes out, like when we were cornered during the war. We can pull together if we want to, but in practice it's got to be made worth your while to do it. Something's got to happen – the government has got to make it

worthwhile for us to work together again.

'Hard work' and 'self-sacrifice' are powerful components of the ethics of 'self-made' men and it is not surprising that they should emphasise these virtues. They believe that individuals will pull together and make the necessary self-sacrifice if given the necessary motivation. Since trade unions and the welfare state have undermined the will to work these must be cut back if the work ethic is to be restored. The need to work was stressed by one of the owner-directors,

> The attitude to work has declined throughout this country hasn't it? Why are the Germans so successful? Because they're industrious and they work very hard and they're very inventive. We spend our time in this country being greedy and jealous that one group has got a bit more than another. I would like to see a leading politician make a series of speeches up and down the country to tell workers that the way to get more money is to *produce* it. Produce the work and get on with it!

This, then, is part of the solution but much more has to be done. The family needs to regain many of the traditional functions which it has passed to the state. It must again instil self-discipline in children and prepare them for hard work in later life. Generally, the family is regarded as preferable to the state and more basic than other institutions; it guarantees law and order, cultivates self-discipline and provides a context within which the strong help the weak. It is not surprising, then, that the family *business* should be seen as the best solution for the country's economic problems. This was aptly summed up by owner-director Desmond Reid,

> Small is beautiful. Generally speaking, the small unit, where personal touch, personal initiative and personal responsibility show up all the time, is the best kind of set-up. It's very natural and right that everything possible that can grow from smaller beginnings and exist on the smaller rather than the larger scale, should do so. It's healthy from the business point of view, from the employment point of view, from the social point of view, and from the national point of view. It's healthy that initiative should show and initiative won't show in anything like the same way in a very big outfit as it will in the small one . . . for the growth of human endeavour comes that way.

This is how small business proprietors see the world. Do these views offer possibilities for a new economic and social order or are they merely a retreat into the past? Before we address ourselves to this question in our concluding chapter we probe more deeply into the concrete experiences that shape the attitudes of business proprietors. We do this to give examples of 'whole personalities', rather than extracting — as we have done throughout this book — their attitudes towards *specific* issues. In this way, we hope to show how biographical experiences influence their opinions.

Notes

1. Middle-class frustrations on these issues are discussed in P. Hutber, *The Decline and Fall of the Middle Class* (London, 1976), and in the various contributions in R. King and N. Nugent (eds.), *Respectable Rebels* (London, 1979).

2. See, for example, the discussions in P. Beharrell and G. Philo (eds.), *Trade Unions and the Media* (London, 1977).

3. Many of the anxieties are reflected in the discussions in P. Hutber (ed.), *What's Wrong with Britain?* (London, 1978).

9 BUSINESS EXPERIENCE AND PERSONAL BELIEFS: FIVE PORTRAITS

This chapter focuses upon five businessmen. This is to illustrate the diversity of attitudes and experiences that we found among those we interviewed. We have chosen people from each of our four categories of proprietor — the self-employed, small employers, owner-controllers and owner-directors. In these accounts we allow them a greater opportunity to speak for themselves although we have edited the interviews in order to highlight the sharp contrasts in opinions and practices that exist among those who, through either necessity or choice, run their own businesses.

Stan Holmes (Self-employed)

Stan Holmes is typical of many of the self-employed we interviewed. He is not committed to business growth and is very reluctant to employ labour. For him, to provide a good service to his customers is as important as making a profit. In this way he is not a businessman in the conventional sense of the word, and yet he is typical of many thousands of the self-employed who make a living in modern society, as shopkeepers, craftsmen, artisans and 'freelance' professionals. In a sentence, such people prefer personal autonomy and independence to the grip of the employment relationship, whether it be as employers or employees.

Stan Holmes is one of seven farm labourer's children. His childhood was hard and, as a result, his education at the local school suffered,

> I had a very poor education. I was very backward at school — and I'll tell you why. As a boy of nine I used to have to get up at 5.30 a.m., go to the farm, milk ten cows by hand, take them about two miles down to the marshes and then be in school by 9 o'clock! Same thing when I left school — I had to be at work from 3.30 p.m. to 5.30 p.m. You just can't learn and work them hours. You were just wacked out when you went to school. And you didn't get a halfpenny for it! You *had* to do it otherwise your father got the sack!

He left school at 14 to become a farm worker. His first wage was ten shillings and sixpence (52½p) for a 52-hour week. Of this, he kept only one shilling and one penny (5½p); the rest went to help keep the family. 'Can you imagine people *today* paying out 90 per cent of their wages to their mother?' Stan's life, both in the village and on the farm, consisted of a disciplined and hierarchical social order in which people 'knew their place'. Looking back in 1979, he regards this as not altogether a bad thing. 'It didn't hurt anybody really. In fact, it was good training.' He claims,

> If my father told me to go and dig the potatoes, there was no argument, you went and done it! When the squire or farmer came along you had to stand and raise your hat to him. Same for the vicar and schoolmaster. You had to respect everybody for what they were. They had what we call 'a pecking order' and you had to treat people as such. If you didn't — look out!

After six years' wartime service with the RAF, he found that farm wages were too low to support his wife and two children and so he tried various better-paid, manual jobs. By the early 1960s he was doing the lion's share of the work in a small firm which was 'going downhill',

> I was doing the boss's work for him but I wasn't getting the end product was I? I was doing all the pricing and supervising and just getting a week's wage — he was sitting in his office doing nothing!

So, like many of the small businessmen we interviewed, there was an element of resentment towards making money for an employer. This was an important reason for his decision to go into a partnership with another disgruntled workmate. Seventeen years later, he and his partner are still in business, although it had been 'touch and go' at the beginning of the venture,

> I was getting in a state. If I hadn't pulled myself together I'd have had a nervous breakdown. I was slogging my guts out to get a living. I was so keen — my legs were like jelly! And then there was the paper-work at nights. It really got me down for a bit.

Over the years, however, the partnership has managed to attract a steady flow of business such that it is now firmly established in the locality. There has been little expansion. Indeed, this has *never* been part of the plan,

> I'm more than pleased the way things are. We'll never be million-
> aires — we're not ambitious. Our aim is just to plod along and give a
> personal service. We could have been a big firm by now but we had
> no intentions of getting big. It just wasn't worth the bother. I've
> only got six years before retirement and I'm more than happy as we
> are.

The main attractions of such a business are certainly not monetary,
although it has 'to make a bob or two' in order to be worthwhile,

> Obviously we make money. There'd be no object in running the
> business without that. But we also thoroughly enjoy doing it. We
> meet so many people and we have a laugh and joke with them. It's
> the *personal attention* we like to give — that's the main thing.

This, then, is the key to the business; the customer relationship,

> We try to run the business as a social affair. We've known our cus-
> tomers all our life and they know us. We're on christian name terms
> and we give them personal attention and they appreciate that. What-
> ever they want done, we do it. They are our 'boss'. I worry if we let
> somebody down — it's not fair, it's not *business*. We rely on our cus-
> tomers and they rely on us. They've given us custom for seventeen
> years and we have to honour that. Our duty is to give a service —
> and this is what people don't get today from so many firms.

As Stan Holmes says, his business is truly a social affair; friends are
customers and vice versa — the two are inextricably interconnected and,
in fact, indistinguishable. Within such a context he and his partner run
the business in an unambitious fashion. The occasional worker will
only be reluctantly employed if the demands of customers become so
great that the two of them cannot cope. Consequently, employing
labour is regarded as a nuisance rather than a means for generating
further profits. Both partners pay themselves a weekly wage and any
trading surplus at the end of the year is taken out of the business and
invested in a building society. The use of credit is scrupulously avoided:
'Ever since we started our principle has been to pay as we go. What we
can't pay for, we don't have. My parents taught me that and we preach
it now. We run the business so that it pays for itself and we live accord-

ingly.' 'Living accordingly' means a sober standard of living for him and his wife. They live in a modestly decorated bungalow and have two weeks' holiday a year ('When we stop working there's no money coming in is there?') His hobbies are gardening and bird breeding, and both he and his wife are active on the Parish Council and one or two other local committees.

In essence, the business is based upon disciplined hard work in order to provide a good service at a fair price for customers. This is interwoven with a tightly-knit, locally-based set of relationships which fosters social obligations. It is from this context that Stan Holmes observes the troubles and uncertainties of the modern industrial economy,

> In my view the country's got to a state now where there's too many chiefs and not enough indians. There's so many people in clerical work — which is unproductive. There's got to be workmen; it can't all be done on paper. People that *work* have to be recognised. Look at the farm labourer, he does a highly skilled and bloody dangerous job and I think he should be properly rewarded. You see, there's not enough *production* and too much *administration*. Take us, for example, we cost the country nothing in administration. We do most of it for nothing ourselves at home! Look at the Council. One of my brothers works there. In one department they used to have 105 workmen and 10 in the office. Now they've got 56 in the office and 12 workmen. That just doesn't make sense, does it?

For him, an imbalance in the distribution of the labour force is aggravated by a disturbing change in the attitude towards work,

> We take a great pride and a great satisfaction in what we do. We don't just say 'Oh bugger it, that'll do', we take pride in it. Most people today haven't got that pride — that's the trouble. They go to work Monday morning and they say 'Roll on Friday' to get their bloody pay! Now what an attitude to go to work with! They're not going to *work* are they? They're just leaving home and going somewhere else and then coming back again!

It's this failure of workers to 'turn in a fair day's work' that lies at the · root of Britain's problems; for the country — like any business — must pay its way.

You can't pay a person more than he earns — it's as simple as that: And the sooner the country realises that the better. It doesn't matter if you pay me £100 a week providing I earn the country £120. That's the only way anybody can run. You've got to accept this as fact. But today, everybody wants £120 and only earns £80. People don't put a day's work in. It just can't go on!

In itself, this statement is interesting because of the awareness that workers must, inevitably, produce more than they are paid. There has to be a surplus and as far as the country is concerned this is absolutely necessary. However, it was Stan Holmes's *resentment* of this aspect of the employer-employee relationship which led him to set up his own business.

His knowledge of 'the nation' and its 'problems' are largely derived from television and newspapers. Nowhere is this more clearly illustrated than in his views on trade unions which, in fact, have had little direct impact upon his own working life,

I'm not anti-trade unions but I think they've got too strong. When they first started they did a wonderful job but I don't honestly see why they should get so involved today in management — it only causes discontent. I don't think firms should disclose their profits to the unions. Trade unions should see their men get a fair wage. It's not their job to find out what the governor is getting. If he's getting ten times as much as the workmen, fair enough! He's gambled! I gambled in this business didn't I? You gamble in life, it's as simple as that, so you're entitled to a reward. Then again, people don't realise — out of that money he earns — he's paying 90 per cent bloody tax. He's helping the country more than he's helping himself! And if some of it wasn't paid back into the business the workmen wouldn't have a job, would they? Millions of pounds are paid back into firms to keep people employed!

The 'anti-social' behaviour of trade unions is largely explained by the fact that they are led by a handful of 'Communist cranks' who gain control because most union members never go to a meeting. The 'trouble-making minority' argument is popular in media accounts of industrial relations and it has clearly affected the way in which Stan Holmes interprets the role of trade unions. Further, they are seen to have had a 'corrosive' influence upon a prior economic and social order in which people knew their place, and where trade unions asked for a fair wage and little more. He equates this 'traditional order' with his own village childhood and his wartime experience in the armed forces, when – by contrast to the present – discipline, authority and asceticism were more pronounced.

> When we were kids we never left the village. But we were never bored because we created our own interests. They haven't got that ability today and that's the biggest bugbear I have. Kids today – there's too much laid on for them. We had to learn how to play. We played hopscotch in the road – we didn't go around blowing people's cars up. To be honest with you, as a boy I was the biggest little daredevil on earth. I got the cane twice a day at school! But it was only fun! Not the malicious damage you get today. You see people banging a policeman over the head today; if we'd see a policeman we'd run a mile. He was it! He was a cock turkey! When we were kids, every man was called by his surname. If you worked for somebody it was Holmes do this, Holmes do that – yes sir, no sir, three bags full sir! It was as simple as that! But today they don't. There's no boss I know of now that calls his workmen by their surnames so therefore they must have got to a more even part mustn't they? I think there should be a certain difference. I think you should let people know who's governor . . . There's no discipline today . . . You've still got to have a certain amount of ranking, because if you don't you're going back to the communists or whatever. I think things have gone a little too far if anything, because, as I say with the unions today, you're not a governor. You can't sack a man if he doesn't behave himself, which is wrong. I mean if you've got a man working who's no good – you say to him tomorrow, 'We don't think you're good enough, we don't want you.' He can take us up for unfair dismissal! Well why, why? If he's not good enough, he's not earning us money, he's no good to us is he?

He sees little hope for the future unless hierarchy and inequalities are restored since only then will owners, managers and workers be able to co-operate and 'get on with it'. These are also necessary if individuals are to seize the opportunities that exist for self-advancement by working hard and exercising self-discipline,

> People pick their own jobs – they're not forced into it. I wasn't forced into farming or the RAF or this business. There's opportunities for everybody today. If they look for them, they're there! If

anybody's got the *will* today to get on they *can* get on – provided they're prepared to work hard and be fair and reliable. I don't want to be big-headed but I think we've moved up the scale a bit. I started at the very bottom but I consider I've worked my way up the ladder a fair way. And the reason I got on is because I had it hard! I was taught the rights and wrongs of life.

Needless to say, in this disciplined and hard-working future, unions become superfluous because employers and employees will exchange 'a fair day's work for a fair day's pay' recognising each other's interests and mutual obligations, as they should,

> Nobody can run a country when, all the time, you've got people in unions saying 'I *won't* do this.' I don't care what country it is – if you haven't got *discipline*, you can't run it. When I left the RAF I went to work for a chap who told me 'All I want from you is a fair day's work for a fair day's pay.' I've always borne that in mind – and it's not a bad attitude is it?

If, however, the country's difficulties are attributed to labour relations, Stan Holmes has personally resolved this problem by remaining *self-employed*.

Barry Small (Small Employer)

Barry Small is typical of those who 'run' small businesses and work alongside their employees. In this way, it is possible to exercise a maximum degree of control over the behaviour of workers without the problems of delegation. This, however, entails heavy personal costs since most of the paper-work has to be done in the evenings and the business becomes heavily dependent upon the (often) unpaid involvement of wives. Consequently, all family, leisure and spending activities are subordinated to the needs of work and the business. In a sense, small employers of this kind are 'trapped'; while obligations to well-established customers prevent them from reducing their activities and becoming self-employed, fears of delegation and doubts about managerial competence inhibit the recruitment of more employees and thus, business growth.

Barry Small runs a small business which employs four men and has an annual turnover of £140,000. The business was originally set up as a partnership in 1961 when he and a workmate became generally 'dissatisfied' with the firm they were working for. As the business developed, however, the partnership proved unworkable,

> Within twelve months of setting up, the thing had snowballed – we were securing more and more work. I did all the costing and accounts *and* a day's work. It became more and more apparent that I was the key figure and my partner was quite content to do his bit of manual work and leave the rest to me. Then my wife was obviously more involved and his wife wasn't doing anything. It led, in the end, to a certain amount of discontent and we finally decided to part company.

Consequently, he bought out his partner and established the business as one which, he feels, 'is known in this part of the world for a very high standard of work at a very reasonable price'. As a result, the business 'rarely loses a client . . . people call on us again and again'. He has a philosophy of 'putting the client first' and sees this as the major reason why 'we're still here after almost twenty years'. Another factor has been his modest way of life and careful re-investment,

> It wasn't many years ago we were still paying ourselves £11 a week – and this has just gone on and on. But when the firm was in its infancy that's about what it was. I still pay myself less than my men – although we also draw from the bank according to our requirements. And when we've made big profits it hasn't been thrown away or spent on a big holiday or something like that. It's been put back in. We try to use it wisely.

Given that 'credit has never been a problem' we might expect that the business would continue its slow growth. But such an assumption would be misleading,

> I learnt many years ago that no matter what you do with your business, you must plan it. You must decide if you're going to expand, reduce, or stay as you are. My policy is, literally, to stay as we are – try to become more efficient with our 'band' and that's it. Definitely, no expansion.

These firmly-held views stem from a tension between *personal* job satisfaction and the problems of organising and controlling *others*; a difficulty with which all small employers are confronted. He explains as follows,

> Past experience has taught me that with my 'happy band' I can do all that has to be done. I can do a manual day's work and cope. The moment I employ another man it means I've got to do more. I've got to do a little bit more office work and I've got to start tracking round more business. I've got to supervise more so I lose out. This is the smallest possible expansion and it would straight away create a problem for me. I enjoy manual work, you see, and I enjoy it because I've got control of it. If I started delegating I'm going to lose contact. I'm going to lose interest. Something will suffer. There's no way I'd have somebody take my responsibilities, it just would not work. I suppose it's really a very selfish way of looking at things. But then you've got to get something out of it. I mean, I've got to satisfy myself in that respect.

Barry Small's relationships with his employees are characterised by frequent personal contact, yet this does not rule out the possibility of 'leaving them alone to get on with it themselves'. Such a strategy is possible because of his careful selection of employees and the deliberate cultivation of long-standing, 'trusting' relationships,

> The sort of person I prefer is a married man with a family, a non-union man. That tells the story straight away. And then, obviously, he's got to be a very willing worker and he's got to be good at his job; My staff are extremely stable – two of my chaps are '15 year men'. Well, if you haven't learnt to organise and trust these men after 15 years then you will never do. I mean, if I haven't been with them the day before, I can talk to them in the morning and they'll tell me at what stage projects are – what they've achieved and what the problems are. Ten minutes talking and we're away again. I think that some of me has rubbed off on them over the years – it does happen. I've got one bloke in particular who's absolutely top line. I'm lucky even to keep him. I have to keep putting his money up but there it is. He's worth an awful lot to me – he's a self-contained unit. This is why I try to hang on to the staff that I have. Simply because I can tell them what to do and what not to do and I can control them. I've got maximum control.

As with many other small employers, he adopts an egalitarian style,

although such an approach can only be taken so far without preju-
dicing the employer-employee relationship,

> I try to conduct myself almost as one of them, at their level. On the
> other hand I try to maintain the governor-employee relationship on
> the nicest possible basis. It's difficult at times because you can tend to
> talk to them a little too much about the part of the business that
> really they shouldn't be concerned with. But that's my fault – I'm a
> little bit open, you know. We talk about future projects, clients, the
> cost of work – things, really, that other bosses perhaps wouldn't
> do. And it has backfired from time to time. You find you've spoken
> to a client about a price and you've also spoken to one of your chaps
> about it. Then they get friendly with the client and you can get a bit
> of a backlash – from both of them!

Clearly, his decision to stay small with his four employees has advantages but there are also risks that derive from his excessive *dependence*
on them for the success of the business,

> You're always worried, because of your size, that if you have a man
> off, for one reason or another, he's a *quarter* of the firm. You know
> it may not mean much to the man in the street, but it is to us! When
> one's off you're struggling. The other three have really got to work
> to maintain the same level of output.

In the context of a small business, it is understandable that employers
should sometimes feel that employees have given *them* the 'sack' rather
than vice versa. Barry Small's business has recently been disrupted by
the loss of a man who had been with him for almost nine years. ('What
made that man go, I'll never know – I've always been fair and reasonable in my dealings with him.') Thus, whereas employees can be 'unfair'
and 'unreasonable', employers are bound by the restrictions of employment legislation,

> The thing that really wants straightening out, as far as the small
> businessman is concerned, is the Employment Act. I'm not saying
> it should be abolished. I'm a fair-minded person. But the people that
> it is against are the employers. The way the Act is enforced means
> that the employer has no rights – and there's nobody in this world
> that hasn't got rights. All I ask for is a revision to give us a fairer
> deal. You *can't* just have a tribunal overriding you just like that. You

literally haven't got a leg to stand on.

If his decision to stay small carries with it certain business risks, there are also high personal costs if only because of the long working day and the effect this has upon his family relationships,

> I'm always up by 7.00 and out of the house by 7.30. Sometimes there are a few phone calls to make first thing in the morning. I'm normally back home about 5.20. I have my evening meal and a shower, then most evenings I'm back in my office till 9.30 at night doing costing, letters accounts and so on. My wife will often spend probably an hour in the morning talking to merchants and ordering. And, of course, she'll 'hold fort' during the day, talking to clients, etc. The way I look at it, anything that's gained out of me running a business, the family gains, and that's it. But it's not seen in pound notes and wages! Overall, I have very little leisure time – my social life has been cut dramatically. With having to spend so much time out of the house, I quite look forward to getting *in*, whereas my wife is itching to get *out*. So there's a small clash there!

He and his wife normally reach a comprise by going out to see friends for a meal or a drink one evening a week; they have neither the time not the inclination for clubs and associations. He feels that many of those who do socialise heavily are 'good at talking about other people's affairs and sorting them out' but inept at dealing with their own problems. This point of view is generalised when discussing the problems of the country as a whole,

> What's wrong with the country? My pet saying is that there's too many people *writing* about it and not enough people *doing* anything about it. We are top-heavy with officials and white-collar workers and there's not enough people really pulling their finger out. You know it shouldn't be a sin for a man earning £20,000 to be earning it with his hands. There's nothing wrong with that, but what's wrong with men in *this* country is that they all want to go to an office in a nice big car. They just don't *earn* their money. My chaps earn every penny they get – and they're really worth double. But in white-collar jobs, office work – jobs are created for the 'boys' as we say. You could have two in an office doing a job. They say they could really do with two more, then you have four. Not *one* of that four wants to do a day's work, so you're actually worse off with

four than you were with two.This is the way it goes — I'm convinced of it!

This tendency for unproductive, white-collar occupations to multiply into large bureaucracies which swamp the efforts of the ever-diminishing productive sector is, inevitably, linked with the expansion of the state: 'Certainly government expenditure seems to have gone damn crazy — it's related to what I said about jobs for the boys. You know, "Form another Commission" or something, "We'll put two billion into it" and there goes the country's money!' In this context, cutting pennies off income tax is seen as a purely cosmetic exercise which simply misses the point. 'I don't think tax cuts have done an awful lot of good myself. Certainly, my chaps are no happier. Put it this way; I know they can't work any harder, so it's not going to make any difference to those men.'

The inability of both the major political parties to combat decisively the growth of the unproductive state bureaucracy is compounded by their fear of the unions, 'who've been given just too much freedom', and big business 'who've been allowed to get so big they've a hold on the nation'. In this situation, businessmen like Barry Small, once the natural constituency of the Tory Party, now give their support in reluctant fashion, 'I'm Tory. I feel that if anything's going to be done for us it's going to come from that direction. But I really don't give out a lot of hope.' The future, then, looks grim,

> I just don't know where we're going to make the money to survive as a nation. I can't see our decline being halted or reversed. I just hope to God, for my children's sake, that something does happen. But it's got to be something of a major tragedy, I feel, to put things back a bit and bring out that old survival kick. You know, knock some sense into us! It's a very dismal outlook.

The 'sense' we all have to learn, according to him, covers the traditional entrepreneurial virtues of independence, hard work and self-sacrifice. Should we regain these values and 'stop worrying about getting our hands dirty', things might change for the better. This, after all, was what Barry — born to a 'typical large working-class family' — had achieved. Through his own efforts he had joined 'those people who've done something with their lives' — the middle class. If others were prepared 'to make their own bed and lie on it', economic salvation would be possible.

Perhaps Barry Small's biggest mistake was to be born 200 years too late. However, without thousands of small employers like him, the provision of many 'cheap' personal services would be at an end.

Eddie Lawrence (Owner-controller)

Eddie Lawrence is not only the sole owner of his business but he runs it single-handed. Except for the help of a secretary and the advice of his accountant, he makes all the decisions about investments, pricing and the organisation of his labour force. Indeed, he is not averse to working physically alongside his employees when the need arises. In some ways, he embodies many of the characteristics of the entrepreneur as they are popularly presented – individualistic, determined, ruthless, hardworking and prepared to take the necessary financial risks. Consequently, he has diversified into a wide range of business activities, always guided in this by an overriding concern about the rate of return on capital invested.

The fact that Eddie Lawrence has 'made it' was more apparent to us than with many of the other wealthy businessmen we visited. He lives in a large detached house with a beautiful wife, and expensive cars. His travels have taken him to the West Indies, Bermuda, Jamaica, South Africa and America and yet he is only 35 years old. His life-style is close to the conventional image of the 'self-made' man but as we shall see, material wealth has not given him personal satisfaction.

His father, a manual worker, started a business in 1947 which he himself later joined. After several years he branched out on his own and set up another company because his father's business 'wasn't making enough money'. Today he has financial interests in a number of diversified businesses and estimates that his combined annual turnover is £500,000. He attributes his success to an entirely different 'business philosophy' to that of his father,

> My father was doing work for, let's say £400 and making £50 on it – and working on a nil overdraft. My attitude, being that much younger, was that you borrowed money and took a risk. You speculate and deserve to make something out of it – I gambled what little I had. The biggest thing you need is cash and the facility to sleep when you've got a big overdraft. You see, my father had a bank manager whose suggestion was not to borrow money – you'd last without it. But I came in with an attitude where the thing to do was

to speculate in order to accumulate. I tried to explain this to my mother once. She said 'I never borrow money' and I said to her 'Would you borrow £15 off me to give to your next door neighbour if he was going to give you £17 back the next day?' And she could see the logic in that. But I reminded her 'You would be £15 owing that night. Could you sleep with that?' That's the psychological element of experiencing the risk of being overdrawn.

Despite his evident success in risk-taking — 'if you took all my money away and I just had a little cottage I'd still put it up as a security for a deal' — he doesn't want to expand his business any further,

There are two reasons: (a) because I've found I don't particularly want mammoth responsibilities. You think you do but you don't! And (b) because I've not been educated or brought up to walk around in a suit. I don't want to be a clerical worker! As soon as I get back from my accountant tonight I'll get my jeans on and go out to my local pub — it's a bit 'on the floor' sort of thing and then I'm back to what I prefer.

He also has strong views on the tax system,

There should be less taxation and more incentive. We've got capital transfer tax and they were talking about a wealth tax. If they bring that in my sole objective in life will be to filter off what I can on booze and entertainment and go to the grave with nothing.

But taxation can also force unnecessary personal consumption,

I know my accountant's going to tell me to buy a new car this afternoon. It's nice to go out and buy a new car — but I don't particularly *want* one! The Jag's only two years old. That's the stupid thing about this system. It's all wrong. You shouldn't get tax relief on something like an expensive car. It's the same thing with the house. I don't particularly want to move although accountancy-wise I should move because of the capital gains.

To a large extent, however, these considerations no longer seriously affect him since he has no great desire for further material acquisitions and business expansion. As he says, 'Job satisfaction comes first now rather than making money', and he derives much of this from being his own boss,

> I don't think I could go back to having a boss. I mean, I haven't had
> one for 19 years. I get variety and I can have the afternoon off if I
> want to — even though you tend to work longer hours working for
> yourself. But you can have the afternoon off if you want to go
> shopping or whatever. *You* decide. Basically, *you* make your own
> decisions — that's the thing.

He feels he would have to sacrifice this personal autonomy if the business was to grow any larger while, at the same time, he would lose the
personal relationship with his employees which he thinks is essential,

> In the sort of business I want to do, let's face it, I couldn't earn
> money without them. I need my men to work for me: it's a two-way
> thing. I employ people I can get on with. We usually introduce
> ourselves on christian name terms and I *ask* them to do things rather
> than tell them. I mean, the 1930s has gone. I say 'I suggest you do it
> that way . . . ' and they'll perhaps come back and say 'We'd be better
> off if we do it this way.' Obviously, you've got to have an 'up and
> downer' when things are not right. But that helps because if a bloke
> makes a mistake it's all to the good, really, because they realise they
> can make mistakes and you too. Normally though, I let them think
> they're running their own business sections.

At the moment what Eddie Lawrence enjoys most is 'setting up a business transaction . . . getting plans sorted out . . . setting up a scheme'.
What he fears is 'getting to the stage where once you've done it you've
got nothing to do'. To combat this, he frequently works alongside his
employees, not because he needs the money but because it keeps him
occupied. He wants to 'keep busy' because the material wealth which
he has rapidly accumulated does not satisfy him. Indeed, it has led him
to question his entire way of life,

> When I was 26 I decided that I would retire at 35 and buy a Rolls
> Royce. That was my ambition. Well, I got to the stage that I could
> retire and I bought the Rolls. But the Rolls upset me. I only had it
> two weeks and I had to sell it. I lost weight. I was *embarrassed* by
> driving it! So that went. And then I found I didn't have to work be-
> cause I'd got an income from rent and from chaps earning me
> money. I could do my work in an hour and then I'd got the rest of

the day free. But the problem was, you get up in the morning and get into a Rolls — but you've got nowhere to go in it and no incentive. You fall down and, of course, my problem was, with nothing to do, you stray from the paths of righteousness, which I did! You see, money creates materialistic things, but the more materialistic things you get the less valuable they are. Up until the stage where you've actually got £100,000 there's still things you can want, but when you get £200,000 you're not much better off and £300,000 and £400,000 — then half a million: it doesn't buy much more! If I find something I want I get it. I don't particularly want it but I've got it. You mentioned the swimming pool. You haven't got one. You'd love to have one. But if you've got one it doesn't mean that much. It's the same with the car. If you've got an old car and you want a new one you'd probably work your fingers out to get one. But when you can buy a new one then the pleasure goes somewhat. I really don't know whether I'm satisfied or not. My basic ambition was to earn a lot of money quickly and retire. But during the time you're earning money you're so involved that you don't develop any hobbies to speak of. Then when you arrive at the level you thought you wanted to stop at you suddenly realise, 'Well, what do I do now?' When you've spent 15 years of your working life working most weekends and evenings you can't practice to relax — this is the problem.

This personal crisis has also led him to withdraw from any form of community involvement,

I joined Round Table 13 years ago. Five years ago I went through the chair. I joined the Masons five years ago. I belonged to the Golf Club and the Conservative Club, Rugby Club — most of the normal things that one thinks is the 'right thing' to do. I was caught up in it. I'm not in any of these organisations at the moment. I don't really know why you do it. I think it's a pattern that you follow. It's like buying your first dress suit: you long for the day that somebody's going to invite you to a dinner with a dress suit. Then when you start going to five a week you want to get back into jeans. This is the psychological problem I've got. Whatever I do, I want to do the reverse!

One way out of this dilemma is to give children the benefits of the business. Yet even this has its problems,

What can you do? If you've got a family I suppose you can talk about education. I've just put my son into a private school. Not because it's the done thing to do but purely because I didn't have an education and I'd rather him not suffer that burden. I can afford it and so why not? I just hope he doesn't get too intelligent and drifts away and thinks his father is illiterate.

A dicussion of private education brings him on to the subject of social class. For the relatively uneducated but wealthy 'self-made' man, British cultural mores pose acute problems. Whereas he and those like him might be widely admired in the United States, their position in Britain is more precarious. Entrepreneurial achievements must be modestly displayed if they are to conform to the niceties of an elaborate status system and not be condemned as *nouveau riche*. He has anxieties about this even though claiming that certain barriers are breaking down,

Oh, there's still a class system, yes. You go through an inferiority complex when you're getting the cash. When you get the cash you don't automatically come into that class system but then you might not particularly want to because the people in that bracket are not the ones you want to mix with anyway. There's two sorts of people. There's the sort that's inherited money and probably don't know any different. And then there's the person who doesn't make as much as you but thinks he's a lot better than you are. You hear it in pubs — especially if you're in a pair of jeans. Some bloke's got a flash suit on and he'll be telling you something and you could buy him out three times over. You know the sort: they create their own class, although it doesn't go on so much these days.

The questions and uncertainties which plague Eddie Lawrence are familiar to many successful 'self-made' men, in just the same way as his continuing commitment to the business ethic and his resentment of those features of modern society which prevent its expansion. In this, trade unions are regarded as the major threat to business enterprise,

The trade union movement started because the employee was being trodden on in the Victorian days in the workhouses and mills. They wanted somebody to stand up for them. But they've just gone over the hump now. If a bloke's employing 20,000 men you can't say that bloke *needs* to work. If you give him too much harassment he'll just jack it in.

But in order to be a successful entrepreneur you need 'business acumen',

> You know, you can either sing, or you sing out of key. You look at a bloke — you don't know whether he's good with his hands or not. It's just something in your genes, or whatever they are. I studied the piano for five years and I could play the piano. But once I stopped going to the lessons and stopped playing it, I forgot it. You see, you don't need to be an intelligent person to be a business person to my mind. You need business acumen. Solicitors and accountants can do the rest.

And also luck,

> You've got to have the breaks, no doubt about it. There's a lot of luck attached to it. Look at Freddie Laker. He started in scrap metal, then he flogged a few aeroplanes and it went from there. A lot of it was being in the right place at the right time. I used to think it would be easier for a person with a higher standard of education to make it but I don't think it's likely in the business world.

Consequently, for him society can never be equal,

> Once you've made it yourself you know you'll make money no matter what you do. It's in the genes. I'm not being big-headed. If you gave me a fiver and one of my blokes a fiver, I'd have fifty at the end of the week and he'd still have five. You can never share it out. But he's happy — he hasn't had to worry about his income and he appreciates me. He doesn't have any jealous streaks at all because he wouldn't take the gamble.

Indeed, according to him, business opportunities are 'round every corner',

> There's so many things. There's £100 a week to be earned lawn-mowing these days. They're just crying out for them! You can't get gardeners! You can't get window cleaners! There's lots of things you can't get. If you wanted to start a small business you can start it very quickly.

It's perhaps this underlying optimism, the firmly-held belief that even greater business successes are always possible, that keeps Eddie Lawrence going despite all his self-doubts,

> If I found there's something more profitable than this line of business, I'd sell up and go in tomorrow. I've got that dealing and gambling instinct. I think the 'big penny' might be just round the corner — and when you've had the 'big penny' you can't make it any other way.

It would seem, then, that any government policy intended to motivate business owners would have little effect upon Eddie Lawrence's own entrepreneurial behaviour. Of course, he would welcome tax reductions and a relaxation of statutory controls on business conduct but essentially, he would always take the risks in order to make money, irrespective of any government programme whether it be Conservative or Labour.

Howard Crompton (Owner-director)

Howard Crompton's company has now reached a stage that is critical for many family-owned enterprises. He and his brother, as owner-directors, will soon be retiring and they are preoccupied with the problems of company succession; both in terms of its ownership and control. He is highly representative of the owners of those medium-sized family businesses that have gradually expanded through a long-term process of re-investment and which have always offered employees good working conditions, fringe benefits and personal involvement. Thus, he takes great pride in being a good employer rather than an opportunity-seeking entrepreneur.

He is 58 years old and the chairman of a group of companies with an annual turnover of £1.7 million. He developed the business with his father and brother after leaving a large, national company when he refused to work for them in London. 'So that's how I came in . . . I had no intention of coming into it, really.' After a reluctant start, he has built up a diversified company which now employs more than 150 people. He and his brother, another executive director, are majority shareholders in the business but there are now two other 'non-family' members on the main board who have 'substantial shareholdings'.

The business is run in an informal and flexible manner without major divisions or disputes,

> We are the majority shareholder in fact, and we have the last word if necessary, but we have fairly informal Board meetings, and although we do have a vote each, we don't regard it as a shareholders' meeting where we can put the screws on. We can say that 99.9 per cent of the time we may not agree on detail but we manage to have the same policy.

He describes his own role in the following terms,

> I myself don't have any specific executive responsibility. I try and help where I can. I understand the Chairman of a company shouldn't be too forthcoming in trying to poke his nose into this, that and the other. You simply get ideas and act on behalf of the company and so forth.

However, despite an appearance of informality and delegation, he – in common with many others running sizeable businesses – manages to maintain tight control over the group,

> We split the company up into subsidiaries for certain reasons. It enables you to see what A is doing and what B is doing although there's a lot of paperwork attached to it, sometimes too much I think. It does enable us to see fairly clearly where money is being made and where money is being lost.

This personal control in reinforced by internal recruitment. 'Our policy has been to find people from the inside. We've taken people and put them in jobs because they're a *good type*. They're *in* the firm and *know* people. I suppose it's the easy way out in a sense: better the devil you know!' The company is now in a process of transition; Howard Crompton and his brother are slowly withdrawing from everyday involvement but in the absence of suitable 'heirs' they have been forced to create a competent and trustworthy team of senior managers. This is in order to guarantee the continuity of the business, and more importantly, to retain family control over its assets,

> We've got a reasonably good team now. One always feels that you must build up so that if someone is ill or has an accident – or if someone leaves a key position – you've got enough trained cover to take over. My brother and I want to feel that, well, if we weren't here tomorrow they're not going to miss us very much . . . But we

have been puzzling over the shareholdings – how to keep the majority of the shares within the family. You simply cannot legislate for the future and get it all right. It's the next generation that counts in the family – we expect our children to get the benefit of what's been built up by us. Our thinking has always been that your co-directors will, hopefully, not let you down if you give them a good start, give them some control in the business, or a real share of it, and give them what advice you can. On the understanding, that as you go back out of the firm, you'll get your cut out of it and they'll look after your family. That's the simple theory. And we just think with the people we've got we're lucky.

Despite his approaching retirement he is still committed to expanding the company in an efficient and profitable manner. As with many other small and medium-sized businesses, problems of growth are primarily linked with the organisation and management of labour rather than the availability of finance. As he recalls,

Our own expansion did not involve a terrible problem in the way of finance because it's been done very gradually. I think probably the most difficult problem has not been the personalities of the people but having the knowledge of how to get them trained. Having an administrative system which enabled them to perform their jobs efficiently. Getting them to realise the necessity of having pro-formas and procedures and things like that, rather than doing it by word of mouth which you would obviously do if you only had 20 or 30 chaps and it was just two brothers running the business. That's probably been the most difficult part.

He goes on to suggest,

I think the greatest difficulty of further expansion is not finance, although of course, you've got to be careful. Any fool can borrow money, there's no trouble about that. Our biggest problem of expansion is to get the right sort of regular labour force, and for businesses of our size, it's a jolly worrying problem. Sometimes it is literally more trouble than it's worth. Our tendency has been to think of a marketable product which doesn't get us involved in too much of a labour problem. In the foreseeable future we hope to increase our turnover by better production – by some sort of mechanisation rather than having more men.

He associates the difficulties of employing labour with two contemporary developments, the spate of employment legislation passed in the 1970s and the more general change in attitudes towards work which has occurred during the post-war era,

> Labour legislation is rather like the controlled rents; the theory is good, but in fact, the object of the exercise is counter-productive. In the same way you have this employment protection, unfair dismissals, and redundancy. They're all obviously good in theory and good in practice in some industries, shipbuilding, mining and so forth. But in our business it's completely absurd because there is a *shortage* of skilled labour. If a chap is made redundant he gets the money and has no trouble getting another job and you can get to the stage where people are encouraging their bosses or their employers to make them redundant. But that's the whole social pattern in any industry, I dare say whichever trade or profession that you investigated, you'd find people saying they'd got a similar sort of problem, it's not just us. These days people have got no worry about leaving the job anyway. There's no worry about unemployment. There was after the war, that's the main difference. I don't think people are more bolshy, I think they're probably less thick, probably, the average worker. But I think that's a general fact of life that affects everybody. They're not so easy to control. I mean, in the last war people wouldn't have done what they did in the first war and, I dare say, if there was a war starting tomorrow, there wouldn't be people obeying certain rules which they obeyed in 1939. Not because they're less brave, or more stupid, it's just because they think a bit more and are more prepared to argue about something.

If these changes have affected the dynamic of business growth they have also altered the nature of the employment relationship in the small firm. He now regards the proper training of his staff as 'terribly important', and is prepared to send his senior managers on expensive courses. 'It is worth it if you can get three or four good theories out of them', while other 'good ideas' can be borrowed from larger companies,

> A friend of my brother is the chairman of a firm which is part of a multi-national corporation and this fellow — who is very much a thinking man — has been quite helpful. You know, he tells us what they do — what the elephant does the flea can do to an extent. We've been up and seen his personnel manager there who's been very

helpful.

However, in labour relations, as in so many other spheres of business activity, the small business can only do so much. The room for manoeuvre is bounded on all sides by the corporatist state – big business, trade unions and government bureaucracy. Of these, Howard Crompton singles out the growth of 'bureaucratic interference' for particular criticism,

> The amount of legislation and bureaucracy – red tape – proportionately speaking, has gone up from 5 per cent interference to 100 per cent interference. I mean you probably think I'm a sort of mad Conservative, anti-government. *I'm an anti-bureaucrat*, I will say that, right away. But I'm not anti-legislation. Some of it's been very good and some of it necessary and inevitable but I think it's been overdone, and it's obviously detrimental as far as value for money is concerned. No business, however efficiently run, by however brilliant a man, could succeed nowadays in the proportion of ten operatives to one manager. When I say 'manager' I mean general administration manager. The proportion of administrators to productive men has had to change dramatically.

In his attitudes about the country, he is in favour of 'decent social services' and feels that 'inevitably the government must run these things'. But he is against 'government waste' and an excessive state generosity which discourages self-help. 'I certainly don't want to see people starving but it's too damned easy to collect money for reasons which are not deserving.' If there is to be a cutback in government spending, this should be paralleled by a retreat from 'excessive' involvement in the economy – a move which would particularly help small businesses,

> Helping business is not a question of money. It's a question of less interference, really. They should be given the opportunity to get on and be trusted, without the enormous weight of paper-work, statistics and returns. Bigger firms can cope with them better – I mean it's easier for ICI to deal with their bureaucratic commitment than it is for a firm employing 15 people.

But why bother to help *small* businesses in particular?

I think smaller firms, in general, are worth helping because they are breeding grounds for employing people in small numbers. And there are a lot of them and small numbers times 'x' thousand add up to big numbers. And ideas must come from small firms as well as big firms. Big firms will take them on and so forth. It's rather like Britain thinking of ideas and America putting them into operation isn't it? I'm not against big conglomerates and international firms because when life is international you've got to have these people.

He accepts, then, the need for 'big business' and further implies that businesses of varying sizes can co-exist in a complementary fashion; it is only the state which, through its interference, makes the competition unfair. What, then, of the role of trade unions? He has criticisms, but they are more subtle than the straightforward 'too much power' arguments which are often put,

The trade union bosses are just as bad as any other political bosses, or, come to that. Confederation of Employers bosses. They're not doing their job because they're human! They just are not able to control their members properly. So they're to blame not in the sense that their principles are all wrong or they're all selfish but they're like the rest of us. They can't control their wild boys anymore than employers can. They should come under the law a bit more, yes. But I'm aware that trade union 'goings on' are, no doubt, always good for publicity in the media!

His views on the political parties are equally sceptical,

When you really get down to brass tacks I don't think the big political parties represent anybody in particular. I don't think the Conservatives are particularly for big business or that the Labour Party go for the working man. I may be a bit cynical but I always say 'To hell with these devils, let's have someone else!' I would hate to see the Liberal Party go further downhill. I'm not a Liberal in the sense that I support their views fanatically but I'm very much in favour of having certain agreed things like the health service, the welfare of old people, international relations – the things which are of general interest to everybody. Parties should be a little bit more co-operative with each other and have, at least, an agreed objective. Then the Labour Party would agree that big business is important and the Conservative Party would agree that trade unions are important and so forth. The Conservative Party are still probably more helpful for a business like ours. In theory there's no doubt about it. But in practical terms I don't think they are of enormous benefit to us. I'm just a cynic about politics. It's interesting from a distance but I would never get worked up and become a party worker.

Is he so disillusioned that he sees no way out of the current impasse? Apparently not; a solution lies with an alteration of the tax system,

I just can't believe that people who are in politics (and presumably some of them are clever, they're not all crooked) don't really know, in their heart of hearts, that the whole snag of this country is direct taxation. The Liberals are the only people who have the guts to say it. Twopence and threepence off direct tax is irrelevant. If we got more of the money we earned in our pockets it would be an incentive for people who want to work hard and earn money. You wouldn't get this moonlighting and such like. You get it in all sorts of trades, motor business, watchmaking, anything you like. You name it – doctors, solicitors – they all do things on the side. I'm sure a lot of our men do, in fact I know from what they've said, they don't want to work overtime – it's not worth their while. I mean what is the good of earning an extra £20 and seeing £15.22p of it going in tax?

This is a solution, however, directed more towards the problems faced by *employers* – getting employees to work and to work *hard* – than those faced by the country. Indeed, his views on the future of the country are generally pessimistic,

In Britain, we would be better off if the population goes down a lot, I think. It's bursting at the seams a bit too much in every direction. Unfortunately suffering, no doubt, from the fact that it once had a big empire whereas Sweden and Denmark – they've got porn and suicide – but they seem to be able to control the population. You see, France is the only country in Europe which seems very well off because it's got space and agriculture and everything else. We've got North Sea oil and it's been a godsend, if they're not wasting all the proceeds! I'm not a great deep thinker on the future but I cannot think that it's going to be easy for this country in the next 20 years.

Howard Crompton has no panaceas or easy solutions for the majority, but for the minority who want to be successful he suggests,

You've got to be an optimist, and you've got to be determined. I don't mean you've got to be very clever but you've got to have a fairly flexible quick mind to cope with it. Not get worried easily, for example. You've got to be fairly thick skinned and ruthless. I mean there are people who get on very well and they're ruthless in every sense of the word. You've got to be tough, I think. Mentally tough, rather than academically brilliant.

But Howard Crompton is, himself, far from ruthless. On the contrary, his attitudes are the epitome of moderation and 'good sense'. It is because of employers like him that family firms are seen to offer a solution to a wide range of contemporary industrial problems. In a phrase, they give modern capitalism 'a human face'.

Desmond Reid (Owner-director)

Desmond Reid's business has reached the stage at which many companies would go public. He, however, has chosen not to do so since, according to him, this would fundamentally change the social character of his organisation. In some ways, there is an essential contradiction between Desmond Reid's personal philosophy and the nature of the enterprise which he runs. He is a great believer in the 'small family firm' in which mutual obligation cements the relationship between employer and employee. However, his company has now reached the size where it is necessary to have formally-developed management structures, within which paternalism as a form of employer control is of declining effectiveness.

As Chairman and Chief Executive he is in charge of a group of companies with an annual turnover of £12 million. These companies, based in the South of England, employ more than 1,100 people. He did not build this small family empire himself; the business was founded over 100 years ago. But he has been primarily responsible for its rapid expansion over the past 30 years, and he is the sole survivor of the original founding-family on the main Board. Thus, with business growth both family ownership and control have diminished. He describes the transition,

It was an inevitable process. The shareholding, at one time, was entirely in the hands of the three sons of the founder. When they died their shareholding was split between members of the family

— only a limited number of whom would be in the business. The girls would obviously be married to somebody outside the firm altogether. So the shareholding has become pretty diffuse. There is no single, centralised close-knit body of people owning the majority. If you aggregated all the family together it would probably still add up to more than 50 per cent but the family is so diffuse — and whether you'd get them all of the same mind is another story. It's not an *effective* consideration even if it may be a *factual* one. In the last generation, family dominance in management dropped out too. The family found the firm had grown to a size where they didn't want to try and control it entirely themselves. It became necessary to bring in outside members onto the board to add strength. We decided it was much more efficient to operate on the basis of who was best suited to the job — not who happened to have the right name.

He sums up the whole process rather philosophically,

It isn't really a family firm anymore. It's a firm that was a family firm and has still got one member of the family on the board. That's the best way of describing it. I'm perfectly content. Perfectly content. It has grown in a way where it would not be desirable from my own point of view to be the boss in dictatorial terms. It is far better that the staff respect people for what they can do, their ability to do the job and not just because they're a branch of the family. So long as firms have members of the family that founded them who are competent and the nature of the operation is such that they efficiently control it, well fine. But we're a size where it would take several members of the family, all combining to work as a team, to do the job and there aren't that many anyway. But even if there were, I doubt whether you could get members of a family to be that united.

Despite this, Desmond Reid still tries to act *as if* the company is still a small, family-run concern. He strives to maintain, in his day-to-day management of the business, those aspects of the smaller enterprise which he considers valuable,

We would say that we are an employer who endeavours to maintain the best elements of the family firm relationship. We try and maintain a personal relationship between the top management and the various levels of staff where people count as people; and are recognised and valued as such. We recognise that staff are our main asset.

It is the family spirit without being patronising, that's not quite the word I want, but you know what I mean. It's no longer the lord of the manor and his serfs kind of thing . . . Paternal, that's the word, it is paternal without the worst elements that can creep into the paternal thing, that is what we try for.

And rather like many of the nineteenth-century paternalist employers, his philosophy is grounded in religious morality,

I am Christian and to me the only fit and proper way for a man to act is in a responsible way in relation to all the people round him. He's got to treat them as children of God and behave accordingly. That's my humble attempt to live, or allow the life to be lived in me, shall I say. I can't pretend that this colours the philosophy of the *whole* firm but it is the way I act. The primary area of responsibility, therefore, is to one's staff and operatives, for whom a livelihood is being provided through the activities of the firm. To do this the firm has got to be conducted sufficiently efficiently to ensure that their livelihood will continue. Profit is therefore only a tool to enable a bit to be ploughed back into the necessary growth of the business and the replacement of its assets. In fact, the dividend side is a very small element compared to what is ploughed back all the time. For the community, therefore, we owe it to deal with the people we deal with in business, in an honourable way.

The advantages of smaller enterprises do not, however, stem solely from congenial personal relationships. Smaller firms tend to operate more efficiently because financial management is not completely divorced from technical expertise,

I would hate to feel that the financial side had control. The firms where accountants run the show run into all sorts of troubles. They say if you can manage one thing you can manage anything, but that isn't quite true. We get very good advice from a non-executive director – the finance man – and from contacts we have with finance houses, banks, auditors and the like. But we take our decisions as businessmen with the advice we get. I like to be in a business where I am involved in the practical side of things. It wouldn't suit me to be a pure manager with no technical involvement.

According to Desmond Reid, this *internal* efficiency is reinforced by a lack of *external* interference or control. The business has always been self-financed and this confers definite advantages because it has remained private,

> The business has grown entirely from within. There's been no other source . . . This is desirable as long as the private company can find access to such funds it needs in order to do the things that are part of its natural pattern of operation and growth. It means you have complete independence and freedom of action. You are controlling your own destiny. You are not in hock to people who have such a big stake in you that they've got a voice in what you do. We have had opportunities from time to time, to merge with somebody or be taken over. We don't want any of this. We want to go on doing the thing our way. Running our show *our* way. If we go public we are at the mercy of the market. Whether successful or unsuccessful there are risks both ways. And there's also a tendency to try and set things up to suit what the market will think of you, what the shareholders will think of you, instead of running it in the most efficient way in relation to the firm itself and its staff.

Consequently, for him the advantages of small businesses are overwhelming,

> Small is beautiful. We aren't that small anymore. In some ways I wish we were. But the bigger the agglomeration the less personal, and the more room there is for inefficiency and for empire building within it. Generally speaking, the small unit, where personal touch, personal initiative and personal responsibility show up all the time, is the best kind of set-up. It's very natural and right that everything possible that can grow from smaller beginnings and exist on the smaller rather than the larger scale should do so. It's healthy from the business point of view, from the employment point of view, from the social point of view and from the national point of view. It's healthy that initiative should show and initiative won't show in anything like the same way in a very big outfit as it will in the small one.

Given his commitment to the desirability of small businesses it is not surprising that he should feel strongly about any developments which might threaten their existence. All such threats stem directly from *one* source – the state, which undermines the foundations of small businesses through its erosion of the work ethic and the family.

According to Desmond Reid, the state not only employs its own un-productive workers but also forces private enterprises to do likewise,

> There's an enormous amount of work that is necessary to produce statutory returns which are set out in a format that pays no regard to the kind of records kept within a company. On the legislation side, we have to digest a continually changing volume of laws. You hardly have time to sort out one set before another piles on top of it. An executive who really tries to do his job has far too much of his time spent on 'negative' work. In fact, we've got a kind of mini civil service within our company doing what the government imposes upon us. Recently, employment protection has caused us to spend a lot of time taking staff away from jobs for internal training just in order that they should not put a foot wrong and land us in an Industrial Tribunal.

Equally, employment legislation passed during the 1970s has damaged the personal and informal relationships of small businesses,

> In the past if somebody needed to be hauled over the coals, we would always have done it by talking to him straight out, man to man. Now, because of the employment legislation, you have got formally to have somebody in to witness what you've said and at the next stage give him something in writing to say that you've said it. Now this prejudices the closeness of relationships with staff. When you've got to do things legalistically it's quite out of tune with the way you wish to do it in the family firm. But you can't avoid it now because the unscrupulous or disloyal member of staff could take you to the cleaners, so you have to go through the formality.

If these points are directly linked to the threats faced by family firms, he has similarly strong observations about work incentives. The state has taken away the motivation to work by creating an environment which restricts the opportunities available for the individual to 'help himself'. Furthermore, too little encouragement has been given to the *family* as a source of personal and social support,

> There should be minimum government and maximum delegation of responsibility and decision-making back to individuals, whilst still keeping a safety net for the unfortunate. A safety net at a humane

level. I think it ought to be possible for any citizen who, for reasons of ill-health or whatever, cannot support himself or his family, or a single mother or whatever, that there should be a safety net. Then the disabled and the handicapped could live at the community's cost at a level above subsistence, but not in luxury. Responsiblity for people should not automatically fall on the state where families can take responsibility within their own groupings. The Chinese system had a lot of community ways, the old Chinese system. There should be limits on people's freedom of action to the extent that they harm other people. I'm talking about very general principles here. One should be prevented by law from doing things in such a free-moving way that one exploits and harms other people. To that extent, the free economy of the Victorian era had a lot to commend it. But it was a little bit too free in some ways and people were exploited and down-trodden. But there should be maximum opportunity for people to do everything they wish that does not overtly harm their neighbours. The government should create an atmosphere of over-all constraint as far away from the individual as possible. *But leave the individual the maximum freedom of decision to operate within that.* That is the healthiest thing for the community as well as the government itself because all power corrupts and power corrupts absolutely!

For the good of the individual, society and small businesses, then, the state's involvement must be severely curtailed. There must be a return to the market economy where private enterprise may operate according to the dictates of competition; it is a plea for a return to the political economy of the nineteenth century. Indeed, much of it has a familiar ring, for it represents a strong theme within the present Thatcher government. In a similar fashion to the Conservative leadership, ulti-mate responsibility is placed not with the government, but with 'the people',

I wouldn't necessarily commend everything the government is doing but their spirit seems to be angled in the right direction. I think it will take people time to find out that they can do things they didn't use to do before and to change their habit of relying upon the gov-ernment. They've got used to relying on the government, of not realising they can do things themselves. Ideally it needs a longer term than probably one five-year government to do it. I think probably two successive governments of the same colour are needed to overcome the ratchet effect of two notches that way and one the other. It hasn't gone irreversibly, but it's gone a long way in some areas ... The government can only open up opportunities which people will then have the courage to grasp. They can only provide the working conditions in which things can happen.

For Desmond Reid, then, and probably for many employers like him, the Thatcher government offers a possible solution to a wide range of interconnected economic, social and moral problems. But will he run his business any differently? That will be the ultimate test of the rhetoric.

10 CONCLUSIONS

In this book we hope to have provided some insights into the attitudes and behaviour of small business owners. Although our interviews were conducted with a very limited number of people they illustrate some of the essential issues surrounding the formation and growth of small-scale enterprises. These challenge many of the conventional assumptions about those who, in preference to employment in fairly secure organisations decide, often with their wives, to 'go it alone'. To restate some of our findings, we discovered little evidence for an entrepreneurial type solely motivated by profit maximisation. Although most businessmen regard profitability as a primary goal, this is often conditioned by a number of non-economic factors. Among many small employers, for example, a personal obligation to customers and a desire to provide a good service not only determine price levels but also attitudes towards expansion. Similarly, profits are less important for those who start enterprises out of a wish for personal independence or autonomy. Further, the role of 'chance', 'accident' and 'luck' make it difficult to generalise about the motives for starting and expanding (or not) business enterprises.

Equally, we found little evidence to support the commonly-held view that the tax system is detrimental to the vitality of small businesses. Instead, schedule 'D' can assist the formation of small-scale enterprises while even among the larger companies, the tax system can encourage re-investment rather than consumption by the owners. We have, then, no reason to believe that reductions in the level of personal taxation motivate proprietors to expand their businesses; in the final analysis, taxes tend to be seen as a consequence rather than a cause of entrepreneurial effort. But this does not mean that the tax system has no effect on growth; on the contrary, it can shape the direction and form of expansion.

If the search for an entrepreneurial type and the operation of the tax system offer little explanation for patterns of business behaviour, a more important factor is the attitude towards the employment of labour. Some proprietors are reluctant to expand their enterprises because it requires more labour while others will only expand in those areas where the need for additional employees is limited. In making decisions of this sort, there are two major anxieties. First, they *feel* severely constrained by employment legislation. Secondly, they have doubts about their own managerial competence. Many regard themselves as good entrepreneurs – in the sense of profitable risk-taking – but they are less confident about their ability to organise and control employees. Consequently, many proprietors are reluctant to delegate and thus reduce personal control over the activities of their enterprises. The formation of holding companies and the creation of separate subsidiaries is not only a consequence of business diversification and, in many cases, tax circumstances, but also a function of the owner's desire to exercise close control over his senior managerial staff.

In view of these findings, which strategy should a government pursue in order to encourage small businesses? Although we have severe reservations about the extent to which *any* small business policy can resolve the deep-rooted problems of the British economy, in the short term some measures will be more effective than others. As we found, some individuals are 'forced' into setting up their own businesses as a result of unemployment or redundancy. Although many of these have given little prior thought to setting up businesses, they are often able to accomplish this with a minimum degree of advice. Nevertheless, given a high level of unemployment, measures designed to integrate unemployment and redundancy benefits with practical advice on forming small businesses are useful. Redundancy payments can provide initial capital for businesses which can be established on either an individual or collective basis, depending upon particular technological and capital requirements and the expertise of the workers themselves. Organisations such as the Manpower Services Commission and Training Services Division, as well as the Co-operative Development Agency and the Council for Small Industries in Rural Areas are probably best placed to cope with such a programme, although their work should be integrated with the provision of financial, marketing and administrative training at readily accessible educational institutions.[1]

The provision of adequate sources of finance and credit is a further area in which changes can be made. In the personal services sector, as we have stressed, little initial capital is required for starting a business. Even in the more capital-intensive sectors of the economy – as the Bolton Report demonstrates – there is a tendency for small businesses to rely upon internally-generated funds. However, during stages of rapid growth the availability of credit is often crucial for manufacturing firms when investment needs severely stretch the capital resources of small, private businesses. Attempts by the banks and various financial institutions to offer attractive loan terms to smaller enterprises help, but their flexibility in this direction is limited by present monetarist economic policies as reflected in high interest rates. Further, these interest rates often compel larger firms to restrict their credit and thus to squeeze the capital resources of many of their customers especially those of smaller businesses. Therefore, the provision of long-term loans bearing below market rates of interest make a useful contribution to many intending entrepreneurs in some sectors of the economy. But for others, a reluctance to accept credit limits the extent to which these can solve *all* the financial problems of small firms.

Irrespective of the availability of credit, it is clear that many small businessmen need training in a range of managerial skills if they are to run their enterprises efficiently. Whereas personal skills and limited financial resources are often all that is required to *start* a business, the ability to manage both money and men is an important determinant of business *growth*. Very few businessmen undergo formal management training and, instead, they tend to fall back upon the specialist advice of solicitors and accountants. This often creates heavy workloads, because of a reluctance to delegate responsibilities to middle managers which, in turn, stunts the growth of their enterprises. The owners of small businesses are notoriously resistant to formal programmes of 'management education', yet these may represents the only means whereby the *organisational* problems of expansion can be tackled. The alternative is to delegate problems, as is the case, for example, with the interpretation of employment protection legislation which is often handled by bringing in outside consultants who then represent proprietors. The latter, however, remain largely uninformed of the *actual* provisions of the legislation and are, therefore, unsure of their legal rights in relation to employees. This fosters an exaggerated fear of the extent to which employers' prerogatives have been undermined when, in fact, the position has altered little. It has been estimated, for example, that the chances of a small firm paying compensation as a result of losing a tribunal hearing are less than a thousand-to-one.[2] To this extent, recent legislative changes only add to the confusion surrounding the employment of labour and probably do little to encourage proprietors to take on more staff. Perhaps a better alternative would be to develop an educational programme which explains the legal rights of employees and the obligation of employers under existing legislation. If anything, workers in small firms often need greater legislative protection because they are more likely to suffer low pay, poor working conditions and to be non-unionised. Further, if small employers were better informed this might lead to a reduction in the level of 'friction' in the small firm sector. The evidence suggests, for example, that labour turnover is high in some small firms and while unfair dismissal cases are comparatively rare, they are more likely to occur in smaller rather than larger enterprises.[3] This indicates that there are benefits to be gained by both employers and workers in accepting employment legislation rather than attempting to force its repeal.

Our own findings suggest that a reduction in taxes in the name of incentives will, in fact, have little influence on the small business sector. Such a policy is based upon an image of how entrepreneurs are *assumed* to behave rather than how they *actually* run their businesses. Even if the non-economic objectives of business proprietors are ignored, the present tax structure has beneficial effects upon the formation and growth of small firms. High taxes on personal income, for example, encourage 'moonlighting', recently described as 'one of the single biggest spurs to setting up one's own business'.[4] Similarly, high taxes on capital, by making it difficult to take money out of businesses, may actually encourage re-investment and accumulation. Current demands, then, for tax reductions represent an attempt by business proprietors to re-assert their control over private assets, free from state interference. Whether such freedom would lead to greater *business production* rather than *private consumption* is dubious.

Finally, what of the suggestion that the government should keep out of the economy altogether? This is seen as the *only* remedy by many of the small business proprietors that we interviewed. Businesses operate better, they claim, if the government is not interfering in the market and restricting enterprises with bureaucratic 'red tape'. Such an argument finds considerable support within the present Conservative administration whose approach is well illustrated by proposals for enterprise zones which would lift a number of restrictions on businesses established in inner city areas. In Britain, we see little hope in policies which refuse to recognise the integral part which the state *inevitably* plays in the management of the economy. In this sense, enterprise zones and other such measures are a poor alternative to an integrated, national manpower planning programme which successive post-war governments have failed to implement. Moreover, enterprise zones are a questionable alternative because they tend to favour the interests of business owners, often at the expense of employees.

If anxieties surrounding the employment of labour constitute the major problem confronting small business owners, this can be seen as a manifestation of a more broadly-based crisis in contemporary Britain. More specifically, we would suggest they are symptomatic of a breakdown of 'trust' and of 'traditional' employer-employee obligations. Before the advent of social democracy — and by this we mean the growth of political and economic institutions that represent employees' interests — employers could unilaterally determine the nature of the employment relationship. But with the growth of large-scale industrial enterprises, trade unionism and the Labour Party, employers have less control over working conditions and the allocation of wages and salaries. The employment relationship, therefore, is no longer stipulated by the employer and more or less accepted by the employee, but is subject to ongoing negotiation. In other words, as far as employers are concerned, workers can no longer be 'trusted' since traditional worker obligations have broken down.[5] We are, then, in a better position to understand the present popularity of the small business strategy. It is seen to be one of a number of ways whereby 'trust' can be re-established on the basis of employers' prerogatives. Within this context, small employers consider themselves more capable of best serving their employees' interests than, for example, trade unions and the state.

The small business strategy, however, offers no fundamental solutions; small businesses may provide jobs in the inner urban areas, cheap personal services and meet the subcontracting needs of larger enterprises, but they do not constitute a basis around which to re-develop the national economy. The 'delegislation' and disengagement of the state demanded by many small employers cannot substitute the need for large-scale structural rationalisation that is required in order to cope with international competition and rapid technological innovation. If, within this context, it is necessary to restore employer-employee 'trust', there is no alternative but the development of an interventionist state which, in co-operation with business and organised labour, is prepared to plan and respond to the forces of economic change. In other words, we see corporatism as an inherent requirement if social and economic changes are to occur with some degree of social and industrial consensus. This consensus assumes that the employment relationship is not the exclusive preserve of employers but is also the responsibility of employees and the state. While the social democratic approach recognises this, it has yet to be accepted by the proponents of liberal democracy and the market economy. Under a smokescreen that emphasises the 'free' and 'fair' exchange of work and wages, there is an implicit assumption that employees should passively accept employer prerogatives. However, in the 1980s this is unlikely to be the case because of the growing power of organised labour and heightened expectations among workers about the circumstances under which they are employed. Whereas social democratic corporatism attempts to cope with these potential sources of tension in the employment relationship, old-style liberal democracy refuses to concede the rights of organised labour and has little to offer except a return to the nineteenth century.[6]

We would argue, therefore, that the current vogue for small businesses is symptomatic of a society which has failed to come to terms with economic and political change. Britain, unlike many other countries, seems unable to confront the fact that employee influence within industrial enterprises has increased. This has created a problem for managerial authority which, in the long term, can only be restored by developing various forms of co-determination and industrial democracy.[7] By contrast, the present small business strategy represents an attempt to resolve this crisis by trying to re-establish traditional employer prerogatives. Such a policy, contrary to the direction of economic and social change, is unlikely to succeed and offers no solution to the crisis of social integration in modern Britain and no basis for moral, cultural and economic rejuvenation. Small firms will always fulfil a vital role in the economy but the solution to Britain's major problems lies elsewhere.

Notes

1. Examples of work in this direction are recent MSC schemes organised in conjunction with universities under its *New Enterprise Programme*.

2. C. Pond, 'Small Change: Small Firms, Labour Low and Low Pay', *Low Pay Unit Bulletin*, no. 29 (October 1979).

3. J. Curran and J. Stanworth, 'Some Reasons why Small is Not Always Beautiful', *New Society* (14 December 1978).

4. P. Stothard, 'Trapped — Why Our Small Businesses are Still Struggling', *Sunday Times* (10 February 1980).

5. A. Fox, *Beyond Contract* (London, 1974).

6. See, for example, the ideas of M. Friedman, *From Galbraith to Economic Freedom* (London, 1977).

7. For a discussion of developments of this sort in Sweden see, R. Scase, *Social Democracy in Capitalist Society* (London, 1977).

For Product Safety Concerns and Information please contact our EU representative GPSR@taylorandfrancis.com Taylor & Francis Verlag GmbH, Kaufingerstraße 24, 80331 München, Germany

Printed and bound by CPI Group (UK) Ltd, Croydon, CR0 4YY

01/05/2025

01858387-0001